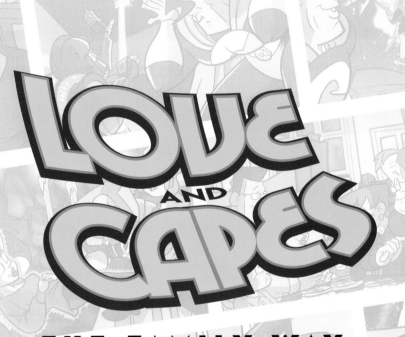

# LOVE AND CAPES

## THE FAMILY WAY

### STORY AND ART BY:
### THOMAS F. ZAHLER

Published by IDW Publishing.

LOVE AND CAPES: THE FAMILY WAY. SEPTEMBER ___ ___ ___ ___ ___ NG. Art and Story
© 2020 Thomas F. Zahler. All Rights Re____ ___ ___ ___ orks, LLC. The
IDW logo is registered in the U.S. Pate___ ___ ___ ___ hing, a division
of Idea and Design Works, LLC. Editoria___ ___ ___ ___ ego, CA 92106.
Any similarities to persons living or dead a___ ___ ___ ___ ___ tion of artwork
used for review purposes, none of the con___ ___ ___ ___ nted without the
permission of Idea and Design Works, LLC___ ___ ___ ublishing does not read or
accept unsolicited submiss___ ___ ___ ___ ries, or artwork.

ISBN 978-1-68405-614-9   23 22 21 20   1 2 3 4

# INTRODUCTION

I've been a fan of Thom Zahler's comic *Love and Capes* for several years now. His art is welcoming and friendly, and because of that, you're not only easily drawn into his world, but you'll want to stay and explore it.

But Thom's art is actually quite deceptive. Sure, it has a definite cartoony bent and, looking at it, it wouldn't be out of line to assume his stories will be cartoony as well: light, funny, and fluffy. You know, even before you crack the spine, that this comic is going to be great fun with lots of laughs, and since he uses super-heroes as a backdrop to his tales, you also know he's going to puncture all the well-known and overdone super-hero clichés. His cartoony art style definitely tells you that his stories will be cartoony as well.

> YOU KNOW, EVEN BEFORE YOU CRACK THE SPINE, THAT THIS COMIC IS GOING TO BE GREAT FUN WITH LOTS OF LAUGHS.

And that's okay. You're still more than willing to go along for the ride. You can believe all that. The lightness. The laughs. The very fluffiness of it all.

But, you'd be wrong....

Thom's art is light, but his stories are anything but. They are very grounded in a real world. I'm not talking about the fights, or the villains, or the parts where capes are involved. Yes, those are straightforward super-hero moments, only with more charm than you normally see. No, I'm talking about how all the characters act, how they talk, what their concerns are, what their hopes are, and how they go through life.

**THOM'S ART IS LIGHT, BUT HIS STORIES ARE ANYTHING BUT.**

Thom draws us into his stories because we can recognize each and every character he creates. They do make you laugh. They are fun and charming, and sometimes silly, but they are also somehow more realistic in their very being than you'd have ever expected. Because of Thom's art style, you might not see the truth in your first read through, but there's actually a lot of depth in these cartoons.

Give *Love and Capes* a read through. No, give it two read throughs. The first is so you can push away all the assumptions you've made about what a cartoony looking super-hero story is like. The second is so you can just enjoy a super-hero tale the way you used to.

And you will enjoy it.

Marv Wolfman
June 4, 2020

*Marv Wolfman is the writer of such comics as Crisis on Infinite Earths, Teen Titans, Man and Superman and so much more. He also once let Grant Gustin and Melissa Benoist share a scene with him.*

FOR MARTY "SUPERHOST" SULLIVAN

YOU WERE THE FIRST PERSON
OUTSIDE MY FAMILY TO
VALUE MY WORK

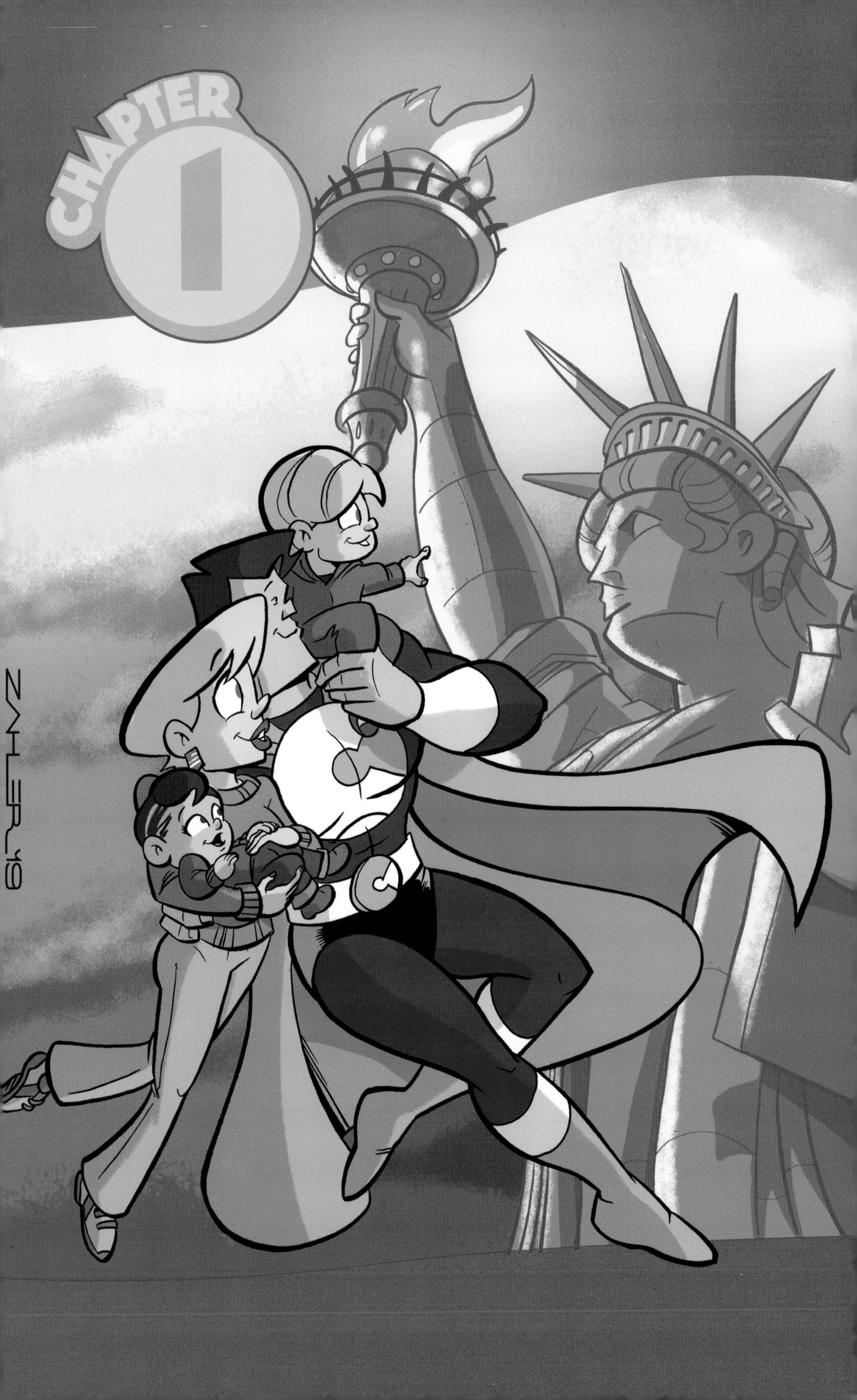
CHAPTER
1

"BEING A MOM IS A SUPER POWER, TOO."

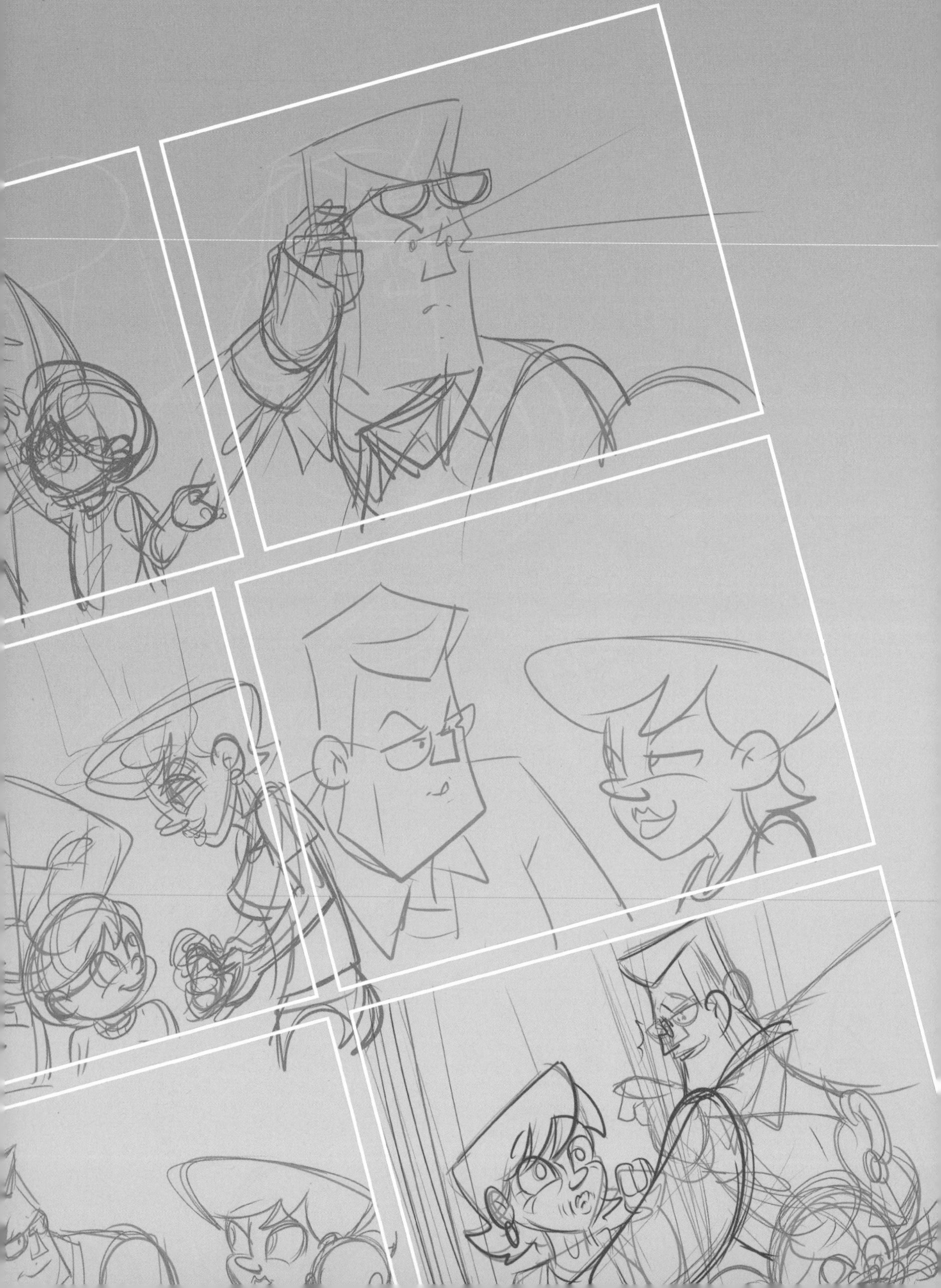

SEATTLE...

We've got a *digital order* coming in--

Oh. It's *his.*

Well, he is a *really good* tipper.

Fine, but I did it last time. I'm *not* going out there again.

Well, *I* did it the time before that.

But you know who *hasn't* done it?

The *newbie.*

THEN...

Are you doing some sort of *viral advertising* thing?

No. I think they're just *hazing* the new girl.

But c'mon, you two. Can I *come in* now?

I've been out here--

FWOOSH

What.

Was.

*That?*

CHRONOPOLIS...

Hey, welcome--

--wait. Is that a *new* costume?

Yeah. The old one got *trashed* when I was in Santa Molinera.

So I decided it was time for an *update*. You should try it sometime.

Nah, I'm a *classic*.

Besides, what would I change? Get rid of the *trunks?* Then where would I hide the *zipper?*

Anyway, it's good to have you *back*, Paul.

It's good to *be back*, Mark.

So, what did I miss?

Headfirst into a political abyss.

Don't get *Hamilton* stuck in my head, Mark.

Well, *Starlet* is finally becoming a full member of the League next month.

Honestly, she was ready a year back, but she wanted to *finish college.*

We're having a ceremony on the 5th and, um, you were her *first trainer.*

We'd love to have you come. And *everyone* in the League would be *thrilled* to see you again.

We both know that's *not true.*

But I'll think about it.

Did *Grant* have any problems while I was gone? I didn't have a chance to talk to him before he headed back to Toronto.

Nope. Everything went smoothly.

Good to hear. Maybe you should have *him* join the League, too.

We've asked, but he still wants *you* to come back.

Anyway, sorry to caffeinate and run, but it's almost *story time.*

That's right. The new *Wally Wizarder* came out last week.

Yeah, we're on *chapter six.*

You'll love chapter twelve the mos--

Hey! *No spoilers!*

DECO CITY...

THUMP!

‡Grrr!‡

I miss my skylight.

Man, soot, too? That's no good.

I'm going to need to clean this before tomorrow.

Next I probably won't be able to find where Abby hid my clothes this time.

Huh. Or maybe I will.

MARK'S Phone Booth

Hey, there!

Did you find everything okay?

Yes. And I especially liked that you found a blue box.

Very Doctor Who.

How are you two?

Better now.

The Little Miss is just finishing up her bottle and watching some TV.

And is Hayley a big fan of *Poldark?*

Yes, she finds the British accents quite soothing.

I'm sure she does.

James is in bed waiting for you. I'm pretty sure he's not asleep yet.

He's *not*. I can hear him breathing. And I'm glad he's up.

I haven't seen him all day.

Plus, we're on chapter--

--six?

*crunch*

You know, it's not fair that you will never experience the *excruciating pain* of stepping on a Lego.

No, but I *will* know the excruciating pain of buying a new *set-exclusive 2x3 transparent brick*.

Dad!

Hey, buddy. I was *worried* you might be asleep.

No way. We have to read chapter six yet.

Uh-huh!

Yeah we do. You ready?

"Chapter Six. Halidore stared at Wally."

"Wally, my boy. You've probably noticed that I'm not dead."

"Yeah. Picked up on that."

Dad, you change your voice *really* good.

Really *well*.

And thank you. I've, ah, had some experience.

**TWO CHAPTERS LATER...**

James is down.

Hayley, too.

So I was thinking--

--we should have at least *two hours* before either of them wakes u--

*ZOOM*

I appreciate your *expedience*, Mr. Spencer.

I was just going to say the *same thing*, Mrs. Spencer.

**THAT NIGHT...**

Abby--

--I think Hayley's crying.

Are you sure?

I *don't* hear anything.

...

You're right. *Sorry.*

This one's for me.

THE NEXT MORNING...

Open up, Hayley. Here comes the rocket ship--

Dad, I can't find my *shoes*.

Again, James?

You have to be better about remembering where you--

Huh. I *don't* see them. Maybe--

Here you go. They were *under* the toybox.

Thanks, Mom.

How do *you* do that?

Being a *Mom* is a *super power*, too.

I'm going to take James to *school*.

Your Mom is running *late?*

Seems like. I can be a little *late* for work, though. You two go.

Oops! Looks like she's *right here*.

Hi, Mom. Bye, Mom.

Hi, Gran'ma!

Sorry I'm late. Traffic on the expressway was *terrible*.

You know, Mark could always *pick you up*.

Thanks, but I don't think my *hairspray* is that *strong*.

Yes, most of us super-spouses buy it *by the case*.

THEN...

I bet she's still there.

Good morning, Jason.

Good morning, Abby.

Has she *moved?*

Look for yourself.

At least she went home. Those are *different clothes.*

Charlotte--

--are we still visualizing?

Can't talk. *Visualizing.*

Charlotte--

Almost there.

No, that piece should go over there.

Then that one.

I appreciate that you try to find your *visual muse* for each show--

--but this show opens tomorrow. And I may not know what looks good, but I know a bunch of pieces on the floor looks *bad.* We--

Got it!

Jason! Abby! I need you now, before I lose it.

Have you noticed her muse is *very demanding?*

Huh. I just thought that was a *family trait.*

Quiet! The *muse* is *unamused!*

AND THEN...

The show looks *great,* Charlotte.

I think we're in *good shape* for tomorrow.

Thanks. Sorry the muse likes to wait until the *last minute.*

Hey, I'm glad she showed up *at all.* The *gallery* is the only thing that gets us through some months.

Making you a partner was the *smartest* thing I ever did here.

Awww. Thanks.

But, as senior partner, I'm now going to *pull rank* and take a tea break.

A *Baby* Tea Break or a *Rooftop* Tea Break?

*All* my breaks are Baby Breaks. Little Miss is growing up *too fast.*

But *then* I'm heading to the roof.

Tell *both* princesses I said "hello."

LATER...

So what do we have today?

Earl Grey.

I was reading about *Patrick Stewart* and--

--um--

Do you like it?

Well--

Five years! *Five stupid years!*

15

One of these days you'll find a *replacement tiara*.

I think my *sister* has a better chance of getting me *unbanished*.

That still going forward?

Hope springs eternal.

But speaking of impossible missions, did Mark talk to *Paul?*

He did, but Paul didn't give him a direct answer.

Been *there*.

I don't know if he'll *show*, but he needed to be *invited--*

--just not by *me*.

How are *you* doing, by the way? I haven't checked in a bit.

All right, I guess.

My brain still goes *weird places*.

Like I realized that I've dated *three* members of the Liberty League.

I get having a *type*, but that's *ridiculous*.

Three--? Oh, I always forget *Major Might*. That wasn't anything *real* though.

Plus, you *didn't know* he was actually a *ten-year old*.

You know, he's got to be at least *twenty* by now...

If I want to date someone who doesn't look his age again, I'll track down *Paul Rudd*.

You know, the part that still hurts is that Paul was my *person*.

Nothing that ever happened to me was really *real* until I told him.

I still miss that *a lot*.

Which is why I'm *so glad* I have you, Abby.

Me, too. We've come a *long way*.

I *wouldn't* have made it through this without you.

Well, I learned *rescues* from the best.

**T**HEN...

Oh, yeah, I see it now. I looked like a *hood ornament*.

Well, I should get going. Once you pay the *toll*, of course.

Of course.

This is the *latest*. We got them taken before James started school this year.

Those are some *adorable* kids you have there.

Well, next time you'll have to visit *them*, too.

Next time.

*Wait,* don't you want this back?

Nope. Not unless I wind up *wrecking* a Buick tonight.

17

DOWNSTAIRS...

So precious!

At least until she starts *teething*.

BZZZT-BZZ-BZZZT!

Miles, you got the *photo?*

She's just the *cutest*, isn't she?

An ordinary everyday angel.

THEN...

That's funny. I thought I turned the light *off* in her room.

Oh.

My.

Hayley?

Abby--

--why is my granddaughter *glowing?*

18

CHARDON, OHIO...

Mark! *Mark!*

Dad, you don't need to shout. I can *hear you* over the mower.

Yeah, but *I* can't hear me.

Your mom wants to know if you can stay for *lemonade.*

Sure. I've got time.

I'm just sorry to take your time at all. A man should be able to mow his *own lawn.*

Dad, it's *my* pleasure.

But, you still pay *ten bucks* for this, right?

THEN...

Mark, we do *appreciate* you coming but you know I could--

Just *stop right there,* Mom.

You took care of me as a kid. It's just my turn to *return the favor.*

It was *no favor.* We *love* you.

And I love you. So I'm *cutting the lawn* and that's *that.*

Children are a *gift.*

Especially *grand*children. So when are we going to see them again?

⹂Sigh.⹂ Well, it's not as easy as it *was.*

James is now old enough to notice when the car *doesn't touch* the ground.

19

You *okay,* son?

Yeah, Mom just got me thinking.

I *miss* being able to fly the kids here.

I miss being able to use the *skylight* back home.

I love seeing them grow, but I miss how it *used to be.*

That's a *parent's dilemma,* Mark. Everything they learn to do is *one less thing* they need you for.

But it's not *all* bittersweet.

No?

Nope. You'll miss a lot--

--but *not* diapers.

Well, maybe you can bring *us* to Deco City for a visit.

That sounds *good.* I'll talk to Abby about it.

And the kids would *love* to see you again.

But Mom... *no presents.*

Mark, we're grandparents. Even *you* aren't powerful enough to stop the *presents.*

I suppose something small--

*Uh-oh.* Abby. Gotta go.

Remember when I'd call you and you'd *come running?*

I remember when I could *run.*

SECONDS LATER...

--oh.

Abby, what--

Mark, what's going on?

I'm not sure. She's giving off a *lot* of energy... cosmic, gamma, solar... but it all seems *safe*.

She doesn't seem like she's in *pain*. Is she okay?

I don't know.

We should call *Doctor Karma*.

Yiiii--!

Called him *before* you. No offense.

None taken.

Mark? Abigail? Why--

*Zounds!* I see the issue!

THEN...

Mom, can you *stay* and pick up James?

We'll be back as soon as we can.

Of course.

Doc, what's *happened* to her?

I have *suspicions*, but I lack *facts*.

Fortunately, that is easily remedied with a *diagnostic spell*.

Housia norva lupi!

You two may wait in the *antechamber*. This may take some *time*.

While the diagnostic ring is *thorough*, it is also in a language *most confounding*--

--physicians' script.

21

So...

Mark, Abigail--

What *is it?* What did you find out?

First, *Hayley* is *well...* hale and hearty and growing in the way nature intended. And she is growing into a woman of *great power.*

Power?

Aye! Mark absorbs the energy of our *sun--*

--but Hayley, she absorbs energies *all:* cosmic, solar and more.

As such, as she matures, she will command *vast powers.*

So exactly *how* powerful are we talking?

Well, technically I *am* required to add her to the *Galactic Watch List.*

I don't understand, James doesn't have *any* powers yet--

--so why does Hayley? And why are hers so *different?*

The answer is hidden in *plain sight.*

Mark's powers, it seems, are tied to his *X chromosome.* Hayley has *two* such chromosomes, which increases her powers *geometrically.*

Wait, are you saying Hayley is so powerful because she's a *girl?*

Aye.

I guess the future *really is female.*

Seriously? You're going there *now?*

Her powers shall not manifest until *womanhood*, but her body is still *charging*.

The *glowing*.

Indeed. So if you'll permit me to *access* the child's nursery...

Ah, this *toy* will suffice!

Peter Panda!

Yes. Peter Panda shall glow *before* young Hayley does, alerting you that it is time--

--to use *this rod* to siphon off her *excess* cosmic energy.

I'll provide written instructions on how to use it *clean her aura*.

The time between such treatments will *decrease* as she ages, until her powers are *well* and *fully formed*.

Any questions?

I'm just wondering *how* to list this on her daycare medical form.

AND...

Be sure to contact me with any other inquiries.

We will. *Thanks*, Doc.

Hey there!

*Mom! Dad!* You're back.

How did it go?

Is the baby *okay?*

She'll be *fine*, James.

What was the, ah, *diagnosis?*

Well, let's just say Hayley is *definitely* Daddy's Little Girl.

THEN...

James is asleep?

Yep. Hayley?

Out and no longer glowing like a light.

I'm sure. She had a *big day*.

We *all* have.

So how are we *feeling* about this?

I don't know. I always assumed Hayley would be like you and James.

It never occured to me that she could be *different*. That's kind of scary.

But on the other hand--

--she's going to be *cosmically powerful!*

No, this is *never* going to get old.

AND...

Mom, thanks for *everything* today. We're sorry to keep you so late.

Please. That's what *family* is for.

Want to me to take you home, Mom. *In* your car?

That'd be nice, Mark. Thank you.

I guess it's the *circle of life.*

Remember all those times Grandma Tennyson would watch *us* when Quincy got hurt or something?

Heavens, yes. That boy was *always* getting into things.

And falling *off* of them. And *through* them.

Crusader! I'm so glad you could come.

No way I'd miss this, Starlet.

You're a full-fledged Liberty Leaguer now.

And proud of it.

They making you keep the pool, too?

They are.

So what are we looking at?

Ninety minutes before super villians is the going guess.

Oh, it'll be sooner than that. Put me down for forty minutes.

So, did you have a chance to talk to Darkblade?

I did.

It's hard for him, you know. Not just with quitting the League, but with Zoe.

I know. But what did he say?

Well, it's hard to tell. It was one of those enigmatic Darkblade answers, you know?

Are you kidding? I still don't know what he likes on his pizza.

No one does.

LATER...

You're strangely quiet.

Is it Hayley?

Talked to Abby, I see.

She *couldn't* *wait* to share.

So what is it?

Well... it's just... she, um...

Mark, *whatever* it is, just tell me.

I'm sorry, it's just you look like a *chrome Pope* with that thing...

*FIVE YEARS!*

SHORTLY...

Okay, so where were we?

Well--

--I just don't like how I feel about *Hayley* having powers. With James, I thought it'd be *cool*.

But with her-- I'm scared. It's *different*, and I'm not sure why.

A superhero father struggling with being *overprotective?*

Nope, *no one* could have seen this coming.

Mark, you've got a *paternal streak* to be sure. But this isn't just that. You were comfortable with James because you *know* what he's going to go through.

But you don't know what it's like to grow up as a *girl*. Let alone dealing with her *power set*.

Fortunately, you've got *lots* of good women to lean on who have dealt with that.

Although, really, you don't need *any* of us.

I can't imagine anything *your mom* can't handle.

So, I--

You made it!

Starlet.

*Darkblade!*

I'm *so glad* you came!

Rule one, Starlet. Rule one!

No hugging.

*No hugging!*

27

I'm very proud of you, Elizabeth. I know this decision wasn't easy.

Your uncle would have been very proud, too.

I hope so. Going full time was a big decision, but I think it was the right one.

It's time.

Besides, you always said being a superhero was choosing the hard thing.

Yeah. The hard thing.

Will you excuse me a minute?

Ah... Zoe...?

Paul?

Yeah, well,...

...I...

...um...

It's okay.

You can go.

But thanks for the effort.

I'm sorry. It's just....

Yeah, it is.

It was good seeing you again, Zoe.

Yeah, you too, Paul.

‽Sigh!‽

Very smooth, Spencer.

You heard that?

Super hearing is a blessing and a curse.

Well, I appreciate you checking in on me.

Are you okay?

It's not fun seeing him. I still miss him. I'm not over him.

But he's still Paul, you know?

Well, mostly Paul. But yeah.

It's just *not* right.

He's a *good* man-- --my *best* friend-- --and quite possibly the *smartest* man on the planet--

--which is why it's *so hard* seeing him be *so stupid.*

# CHAPTER 2

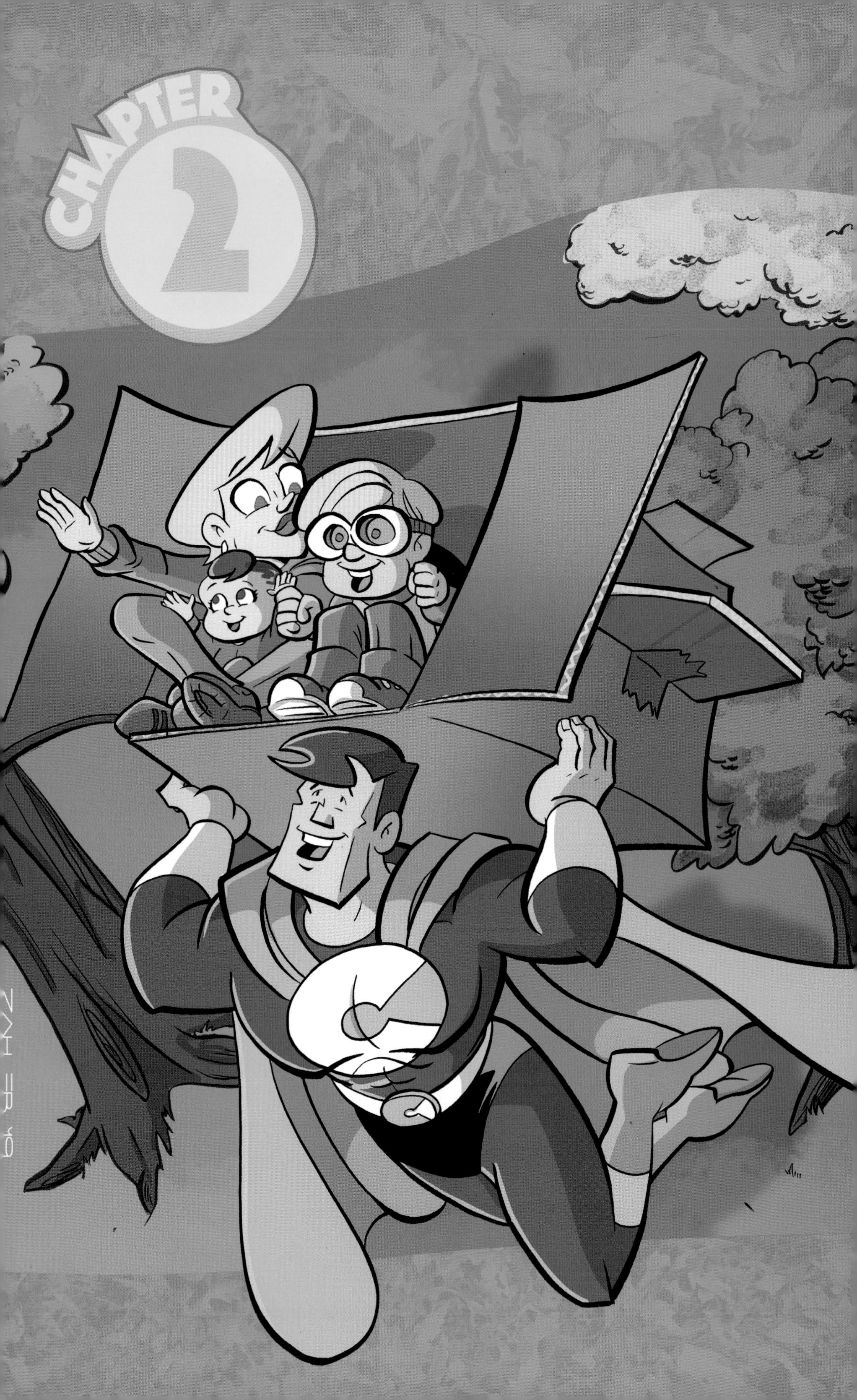

"YOU MISS BEING OLD PAUL SOMETIMES, DON'T YOU?"

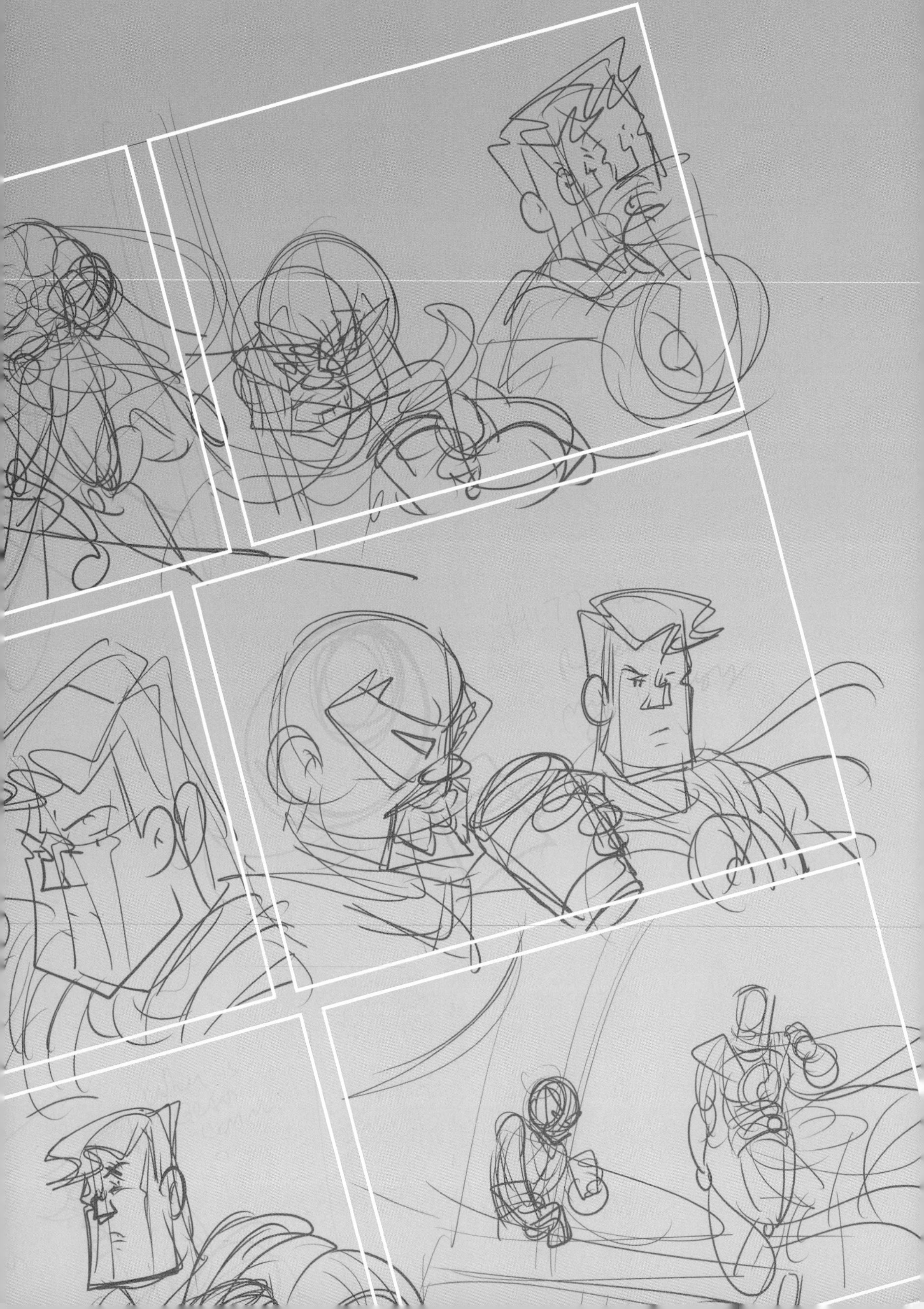

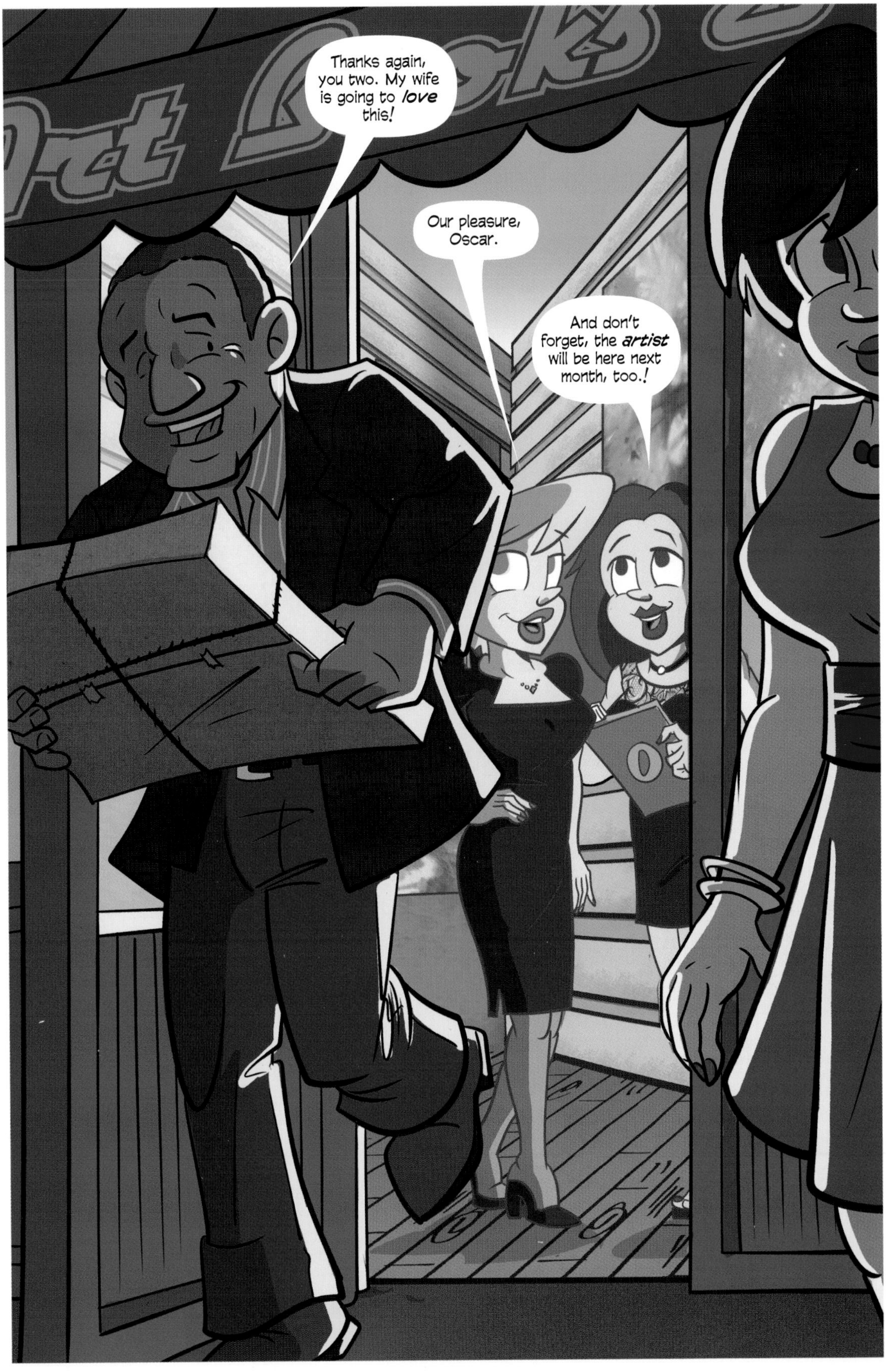
Thanks again, you two. My wife is going to *love* this!
Our pleasure, Oscar.
And don't forget, the *artist* will be here next month, too.!

≯Whew!≮ I love gallery nights, but I also love when they're *over*.

Me, too.

So how'd we do?

Oooh, I didn't realize you'd sold those *two* pieces tonight.

Yeah, we got lucky there.

Looks like we did okay overall.

Of course, you know what would *really* help...

*Don't* say it. *Don't* say it.

*If we could sell the wine we give out!*

There it is.

Charlotte, you *know* we're not allowed to sell the wine. We're operating under a *gallery carve out*.

But if--

--if we get a *liquor license*. Yeah.

Look, I want to sell *books*. And *art*. I don't want to lose sight of that.

I don't want to be a *bar*.

I know. But we're already giving it away. And we could keep it just for *special events*.

You really think this is the *right* idea?

I do. And I'm prepared to help *however* you need--

Paperwork, health inspections, *and* a city council petition?

--*emotionally*. Help emotionally.

MEANWHILE...

Dad! Look how high I made my tower!

Can I take a picture to show Mommy?

Sure! My phone is on the couch.

Hayley!

Mommy's going to be so impressed!

THEN...

Hello, Mark... James?

Mommy!

Shouldn't you be in *bed*, little boy?

I told him he could stay up to wait for you as long as we flew *straight to bed* when you got here.

Good night, James.

Here we go! Now remember--

--think of your hands as *ailerons* and your feet as *flaps*.

What? He's going to have to learn sometime.

**So...** Oh, that's the look of someone who had the *liquor license discussion* with Charlotte again.

Yeah. The show went fine, but then she brought it up *again* tonight.

Oooh, that feels *nice*.

What do you think?

It's your business, and you're the expert in it. That said, it *does* make sense to me.

Multiple revenue streams are always good.

Plus, you'd be able to buy wine at *wholesale*.

**SOLD!**

**And then...** You about ready for *bed*, dear?

Yeah.

Hey, where are *you* going, buster?

You're *ridiculous*, you know.

And you *love* it.

CHRONOPOLIS...

You were a little *rough* on the Terminus Twins weren't you?

Mark, they were trying to hold *Australia* for ransom.

Yeah, but I'm just saying, they're going to need a *lot* a dental work now.

I'm just working through some aggression.

You *could* find a *therapist*, you know.

Beating people up *is* my therapy.

So, when is Grant coming back from his *gap year?*

I think he's going to stay in Toronto for a while.

Oh?

Originally, he was going to lighten the load so I could have more of a life.

But since I have *less of one* these days, that's not really necessary.

THE NEXT DAY...

Hey, Abby. I was going to go on my break.

Wait, it's *1:00pm* *already?* I've been filling out forms *all morning?*

Afraid so.

Look, I was just going to run home, but I could go get Zippy Sub or something.

Maybe you could use a chick-a-salsa sub--

--for that matter, maybe you could use a drink.

Not according to *this* form.

THAT EVENING...

Hey, Mommy's home!

Should we ask her how her day was?

Probably not. It was mostly a day of documentation and waiting at City Hall.

And how did *that* go?

Let's just say I'm starting to understand why people started *speakeasies.*

If it helps, I *do* know how to convert a closet into a secret room.

LATER...

--it's like the paperwork is meant to *keep me* from trying to do anything.

Complexity *is* a barrier to entry.

You have a business, how do you deal with this stuff?

Well, I do have a phalanx of lawyers--

--plus, honestly, I'm a stacked, six-foot, leggy superhero. People usually just *give* me what I want.

And if they don't, you threaten to squish them like a grape?

*Never* going to let me forget that are you?

It is kind of funny talking regulatory compliance with a *vigilante*, though.

Oh, I'm *not* a vigilante.

The Liberty League charter grants law enforcement powers to all its members.

I mean, we all had to do a couple hours of *classes*, but after that, we're all legal.

So it's easier to get *deputized* than to get a *liquor license?*

Sounds like.

On the upside, I don't have to run around wearing a *unicorn horn* on my head.

*FIVE STUPID YEARS...!*

LATER...

Is it going any *better* today?

Well, I've scanned in all the documentation they needed.

It took like an *hour* to upload it all, but I think I got everything they needed.

Gray bars are filled and I've double-checked the form.

So get ready, I'm going to get you a liquor license--

--wait. Where did the *submit* button go?

"Alert! To better serve you, this site will be down for maintenance from now until Tuesday morning."

FINALLY...

Hey! I just got an email from the Alcohol Beverage Control board.

"We have received your application. We will review it and get back to you within *three to six months*."

I guess it's all over but the *waiting*.

It's too bad I didn't submit it six months ago, isn't it?

Yeah, I--

No!

I am *not* going back in time for that!

TORONTO...

Crusader! What brings you to the Great White North?

I'm on League business, *Dagger*.

We've tried to get Darkblade to come back to the League, but he's being *adamant* about staying solo.

So, we were wondering if you might be interested in finally joining us. We could use a *master detective*.

It'd be my *honor*.

Of course, if your mentor had trained you well enough, you would have figured all that out *before* I said anything.

Check your cape pouch.

No way! *No way!*

So Paul said you've decided to stay up here for a while?

Well, "decided" is the wrong word. I asked about coming back to Chronopolis and he told me he had it all under control.

I'm glad to serve where I'm needed--

--but I thought by this point I'd be working more closely with him.

Huh. I don't know what to tell you.

Things will unfold as they should. But, until then, can I ask a favor?

Deep dish pizza from Enrico's?

Meat lover's, please. Can't get anything like that up here.

LATER...

Mommy, can we go after school today?

Not today, James. But this weekend.

What's up?

James has finally decided what he wants to be for Halloween and he's wondering when we can get his costume.

What did he land on?

Kylo Ren.

I'm not sure I'm comfortable with that, dear.

THEN...

Mark, you seem upset by James's costume choice.

Well, maybe a little.

I get it.

You do?

Sure. I don't like seeing our soon-to-be super son dressing up like a *villain*, but that kind of make-believe is natural at his age.

No, it's that he *killed his dad!*

LATER...

Jason, can I run an idea by you?

This isn't your *drive-through gallery idea* again, is it?

I told you, I was hopped up on cold medicine that day.

Anyway, I thought we should go *bigger* than just handing out candy this year.

And I thought I remembered you knew some poster artist who does stuff for the Lone Star Theatre.

Didn't they do some retro Universal Monster thing? Does he have originals we could display and sell?

Charlotte, that's a great idea! That's Ethan, and I know he's got a bunch of other artist friends who could probably set up, too. We could do a whole *pop-up gallery!*

Other artists? Are they all that kind of messed-up horror artist types?

Charlotte, *all* artists are *messed-up* types.

THEN...

Charlotte, I love this! I'll email the other merchants and we'll make a whole event of this!

Awesome!

It's too bad we won't have our liquor license for this. It'd be perfect for it.

Maybe next year.

I bet I could get some *kids' scary story book* on remainder and give that out when they come. Rot their minds, not their teeth.

Whoa, whoa! Hold your horses!

Books are good, but we're still giving out *candy,* too.

We're *not monsters.*

CHRONOPOLIS...

So this is gonna be a thing, huh?

Well... yeah.

Look, I get that it's just play and all, but I *don't like* seeing my son dress up as the big bad of the new *Star Wars* films.

Half my job as a parent is *keeping* him from the Dark Side.

Am I being oversensitive about this? *Maybe.* But it just bothers me.

And he kills his father.

*And he kills his father!*

So, Paul, when *you* were a kid, what did you dress up as for Halloween?

Lots of things. I did have the LaCroix Pictures warehouse as a costume closet.

I was a screen-accurate *Oompa Loompa* one year.

When I was going through my *Star Wars* phase, I was absolutely obsessed with Lando Calrissian.

I really dug that *cape.*

Glad to see you've grown out of that.

And, of course, as I got older, my Halloween parties got larger and more *opulent*.

I believe *Entertainment Weekly* called them "debaucherous."

I was young, rich, and stupid.

Heck, there was one year I got a half-dozen of the Dallas Cowboys Cheerleaders to dress up like Red Sonja and...

You miss being Old Paul sometimes, don't you?

Every now and then.

Hey, the bookstore and a bunch of other merchants are doing one of those Trick or Treat festival events next week.

You should come.

You haven't seen the kids in forever. And it'd be fun to hang out *outside* of work.

James is getting older. I hate *confusing* him by letting him see someone his father shouldn't really know socially.

Then come in a costume. The kids wouldn't know, but I would.

It's the season of disguises, you know.

If *I* came in disguise, you'd *never* recognize me.

Challenge accepted.

**THEN...**

It looks like I got here just in time to *rescue* that other glass.

So, did you get it?

You have slain the Dragon of Paperwork and got your license application in.

Do you really think I'd come here empty-handed?

Klausomann chocolate from Switzerland.

But you could have had Mark get this though.

Yes, but I didn't want just *half* a chocolate bar.

Have you heard anything from your *sister* lately? How is rescinding your banishment going?

She tells me it's going well. But--

--but it's definitely wearing on me.

I *knew* what I was giving up when I chose to stay here, but I thought I'd have *Paul*... a *family*--

--not be all on *my* own.

Oh, Zoe... I know it's not the same, but--

--you *do* have *family* here.

So what's taking Oriana *so long* to change things? You've said there's support for the measure.

Yes, but the Leandian government is specifically crafted to be deliberative. It's a feature, not a bug.

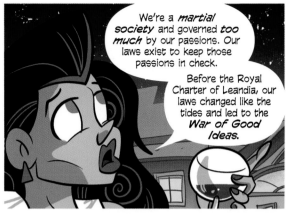

We're a *martial society* and governed *too much* by our passions. Our laws exist to keep those passions in check.

Before the Royal Charter of Leandia, our laws changed like the tides and led to the *War of Good Ideas.*

And now?

Seemingly endless debates designed to remove all emotion from the proceedings.

From what I hear, Oriana is a great debater, too. She won the last one on a *TKO.*

TKO?

Like I said, *martial society.*

THEN...

--so that's what we're doing.

That sounds like a great event!

Can I donate some prizes or something?

Oh, that would be amazing!

I've got some signed books, some bookmarks--

--and candy, of course. We're *not savages.*

I think that's it for the wine.

Oh, no! I didn't even have a chance to compose your *victory song* yet.

I get a victory song, too?

All warriors do.

I was thinking of calling it *"Lady Abigail's Triumph O'er the Scourge of the Blood Red Tape."*

Hey, I got something from the Alcohol Beverage Control Board.

Uh-oh! What is it?

Hey, it's my license! It came *early!*

We *can* have wine at the Hallo-Read event!

This can't be good.

What do you mean? This is *great.*

Abby, I deal with the IRS all the time. This is *not* how government bureaucracies work.

Something is *dreadfully wrong.*

Dreadfully?

Doc, it's Mark. *Which* reality are we in?

Is this the darkest timeline? *Is this the darkest timeline?!*

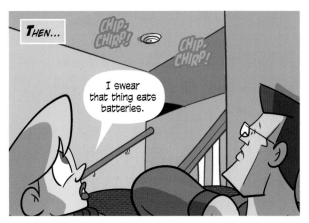

THEN...

CHIP. CHIRP!

CHIP. CHIRP!

I swear that thing eats batteries.

CHIP. CHIRP!

I'll get it.

Mark...?

The smoke detector might have woken up James.

CHIP. CHIRP!

Thank you.

THEN...

Is it time for Hayley to have her *aura* cleaned again?

I thought Doc Karma said it'd be a while before she recharged.

He did, but I like getting in the practice.

Besides, it can't hurt to drain down the tank, right?

I suppose not.

Our little glowbug.

Heh. *Glowbug.*

Wait, *Glowbug?*

Oh, heck, that nickname's gonna *stick,* isn't it?

*Nickname?* I think I just gave her a *codename!*

LATER...

Sexy Census Taker...

...Sexy Captain Kangaroo...

...Sexy UPS Driver...

So, no good Halloween costumes for you?

Nothing that doesn't fill more than a sandwich bag and--

--oh, *hey!* Look at this!

Sexy Superhero Princess

...t for your right ...ndy in this ...e hero ...mble. Includes ... and tiara.

$2.99

HALLO WEEZIE

That's funny!

Though honestly, she used to wear *far less* than that.

The *tiara* is nice, though.

THEN... Oh, what are my boys up to?

We're carving a pumpkin, Mommy.

Yes, you are.

Dad's letting me scoop it out.

And, we covered the kitchen in newspaper, plus he's wearing one of my old shirts. So the mess is contained.

So, care to explain the pumpkin guts on my ceiling?

Huh. No clue.

AND... Dad, I drew the face for you to cut.

That looks great, James!

Now, this knife is only for mommies and daddies, okay?

Got it, Dad!

Because you could get hurt with this.

These carving knives are very sharp--

--um, and sometimes brittle.

FINALLY...

You make a pretty *cute* witch, dear!

Thanks! Now, can you take care of getting the kids ready by *yourself?*

I'd start getting ready at *six*.

Six? Hallo-Read is at *seven*.

And no *proper costume change* should take more than *thirty seconds* anyway.

Oh?

Tell you what, if you can get them ready in less than thirty *minutes*--

--*this* won't be the *only* costume I wear tonight.

Really? I--

--who am I kidding?

I can't even *pretend* I can make that happen.

Oh, well. There's always your birthday.

Hey, this *isn't* a Kylo Ren costume.

No, it's not.

When we went to the Halloween store, he decided on something else. *Maaaybe* with a little help from Mommy.

I got one for you, too. Properly off-the-shelf so no one realizes Mark Spencer has too good a costume.

You're the *best*, you know?

Thanks.

And besides--

--Kylo Ren tried to kill his *mom*, too.

This was a great idea, Charlotte.

Couldn't have done it without you, Jason.

Also true.

Your artist friends really came through, too. We should do more of these themed events.

Agreed. But we'll have to come up with something as catchy as horror films. They have quite a fanbase.

Like me! I love a good scary movie. I think *Alien* is my favorite.

*Ridley Scott.* That's a good one.

What's about you? What's your *most horrific* horror movie?

*Birdemic.*

That director was clearly possessed by something unholy to make *that* piece of trash.

Okay, *everyone* gets a piece of candy and a book!

So, *who* do we have here?

A devil--

--a Whoa Bot--

--and Carmen Corannia from *Wally Wizarder*.

And what's *your* costume?

I'm *Mary Shelley*--

--author of *Frankenstein* and inventor of science fiction as we know it.

Mary-- science fict--

--candy.

You get *all* the candy.

*THEN...*

Hey, I was promised some cute nieces and nephews, you know.

I'm sure Mark will be down in a couple of minutes.

You don't need to go up and help him?

He can save the world by himself, I'm sure he can get two kids ready on his own.

James, put the game down and get ready.

Huh? Okay.

≶Waaaah!≶

≶Waaaah!≶

How can you need to be changed *again?*

≶Waaaah!≶

Dad, I can't find my other sock.

It's on the bed next to you.

I don't see it. Can you help me look?

*AND THEN...*

Okay, everyone, picture time!

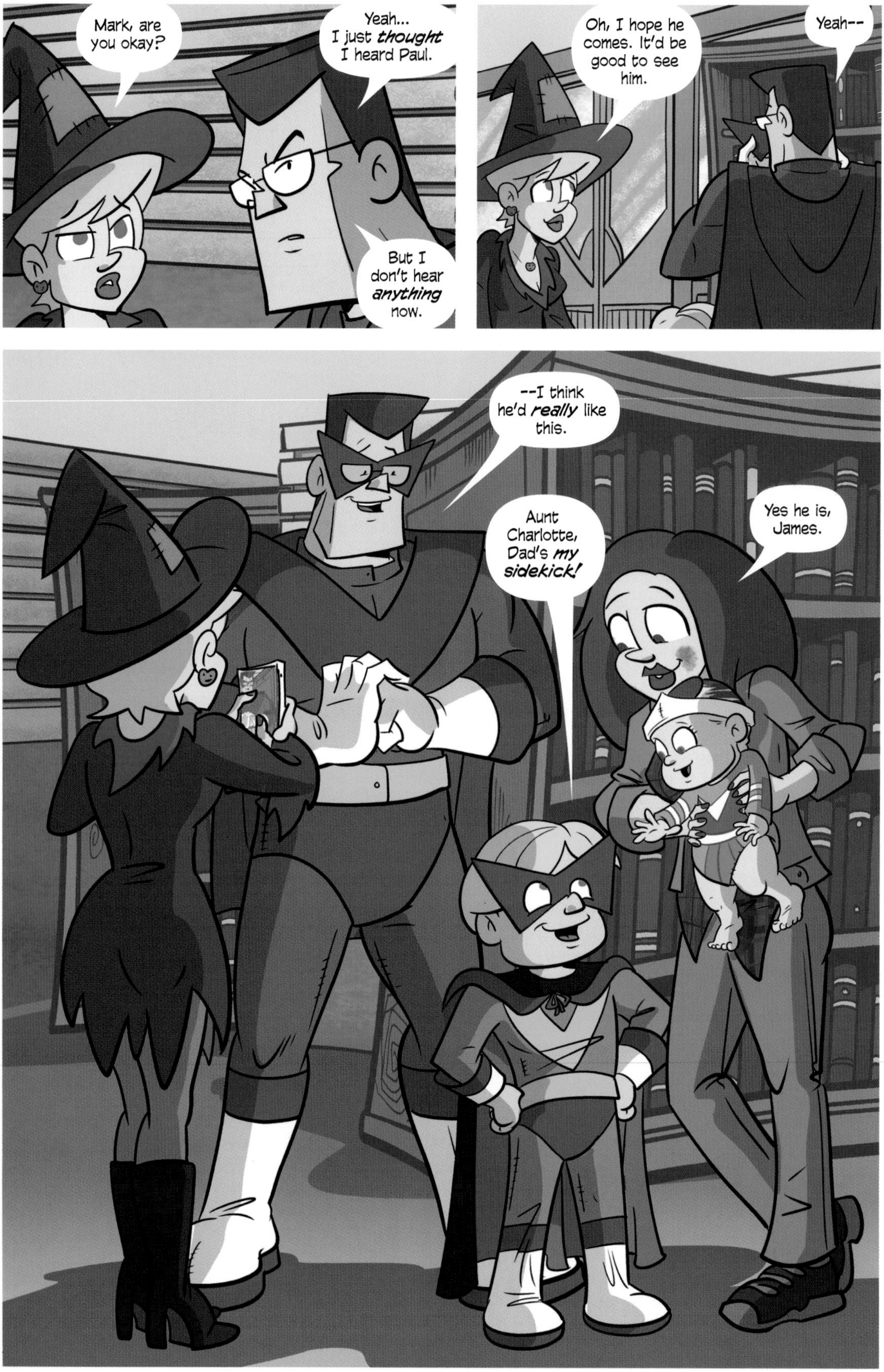
Mark, are you okay?
Yeah... I just *thought* I heard Paul.
But I don't hear *anything* now.
Oh, I hope he comes. It'd be good to see him.
Yeah--
--I think he'd *really* like this.
Aunt Charlotte, Dad's *my sidekick!*
Yes he is, James.

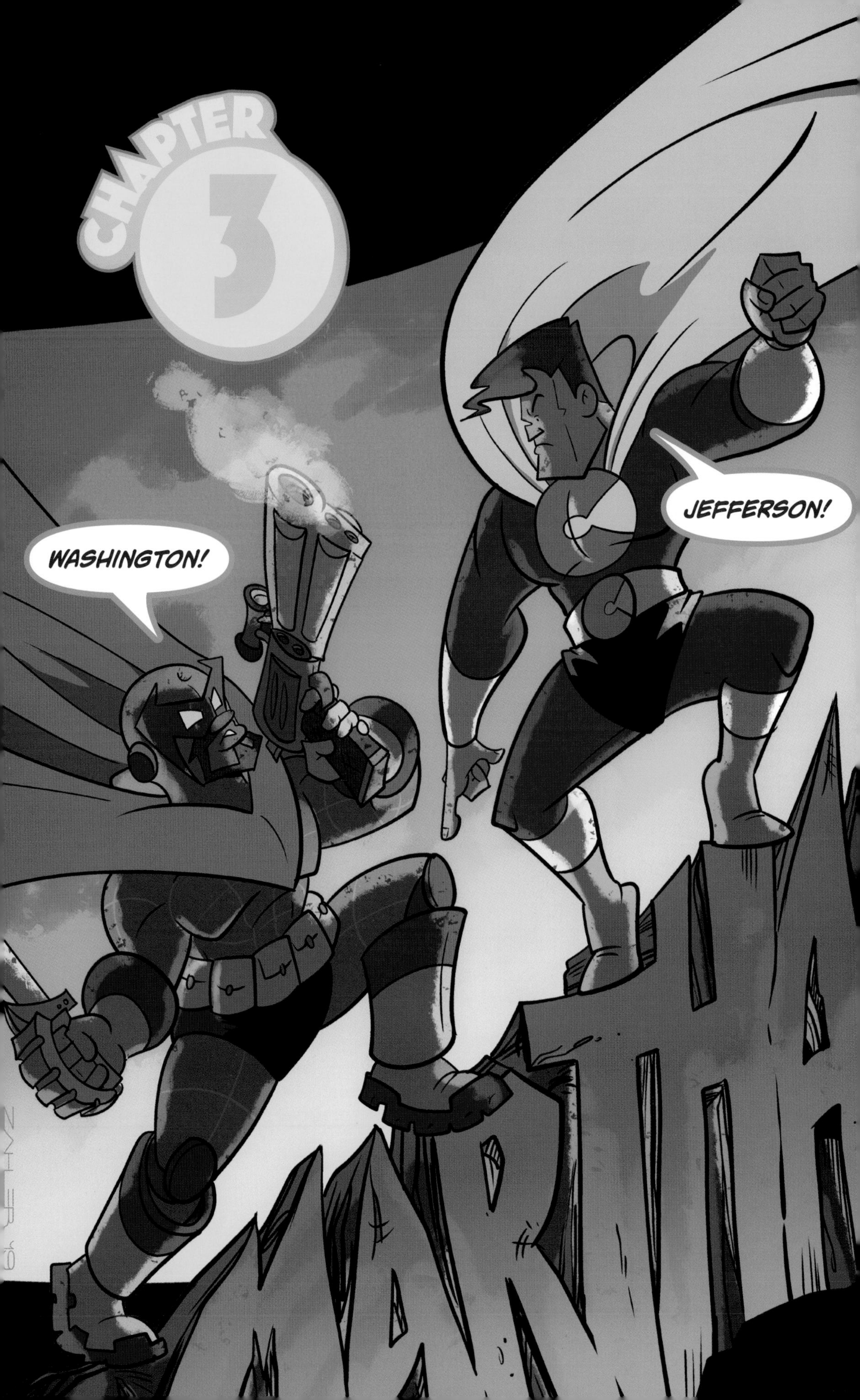
CHAPTER 3
JEFFERSON!
WASHINGTON!
ZAHLER 19

# "THAT'S NOT A THING, RIGHT?"

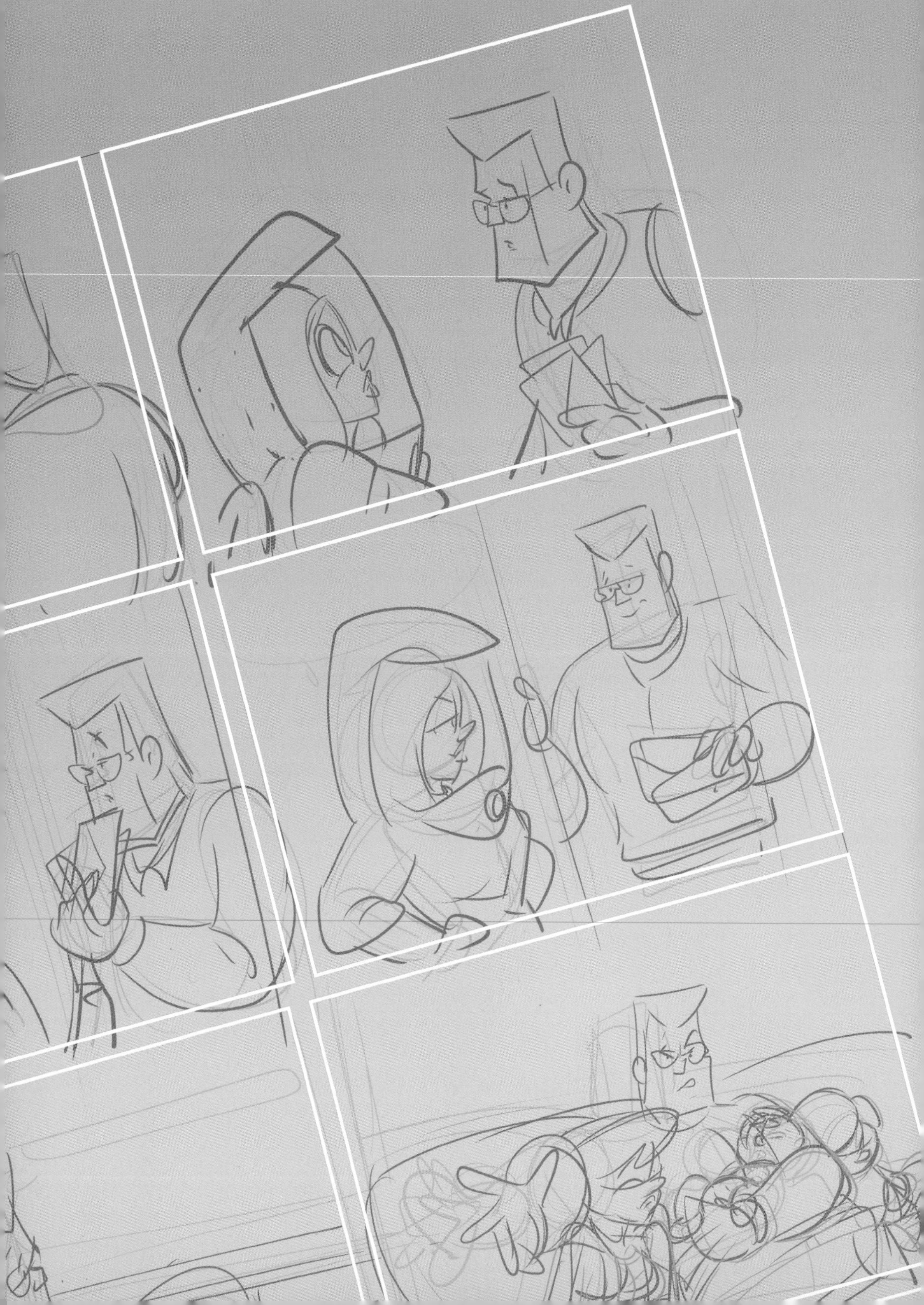

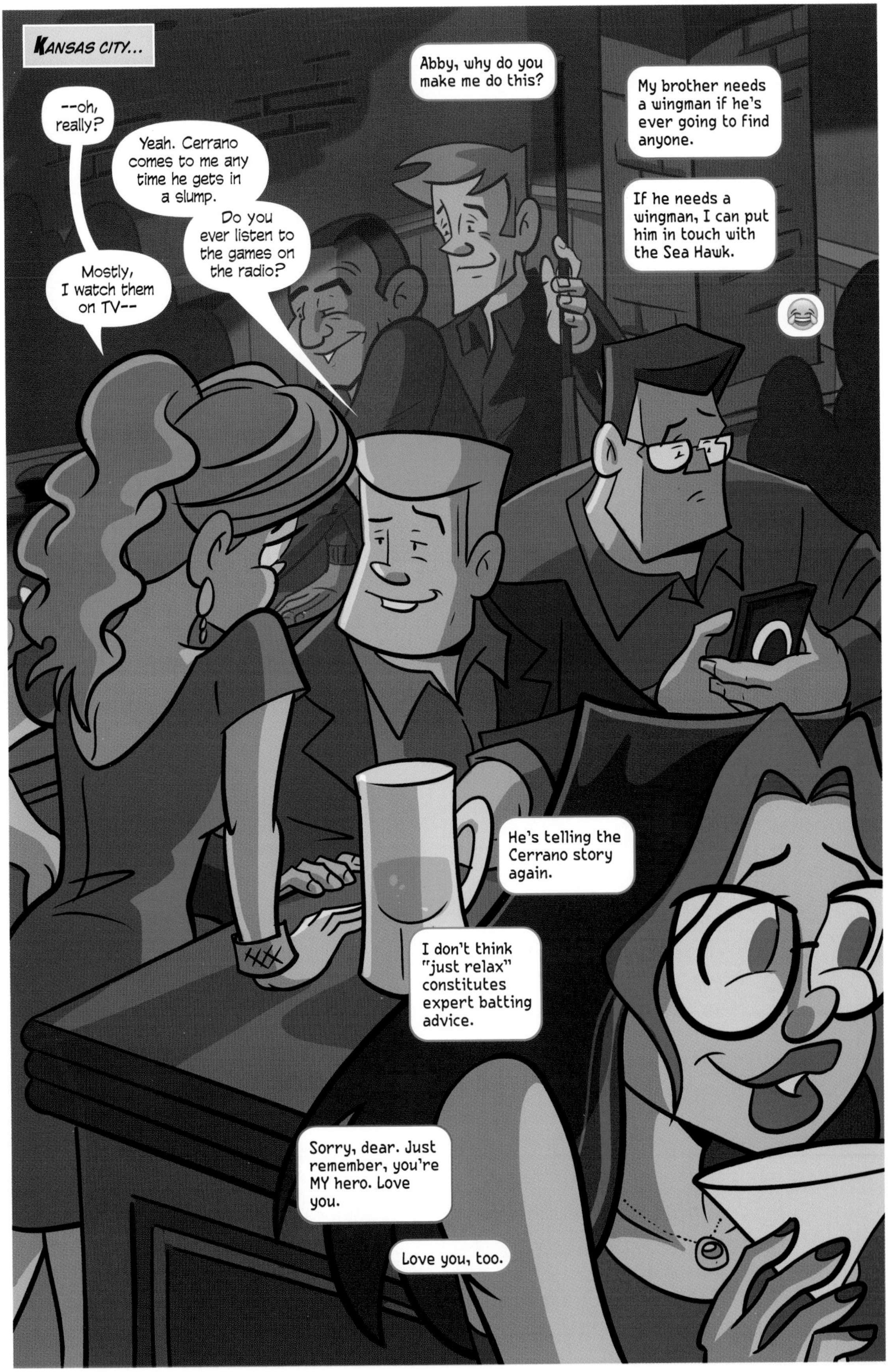
Kansas City...
--oh, really?
Yeah. Cerrano comes to me any time he gets in a slump.
Do you ever listen to the games on the radio?
Mostly, I watch them on TV--
Abby, why do you make me do this?
My brother needs a wingman if he's ever going to find anyone.
If he needs a wingman, I can put him in touch with the Sea Hawk.
He's telling the Cerrano story again.
I don't think "just relax" constitutes expert batting advice.
Sorry, dear. Just remember, you're MY hero. Love you.
Love you, too.

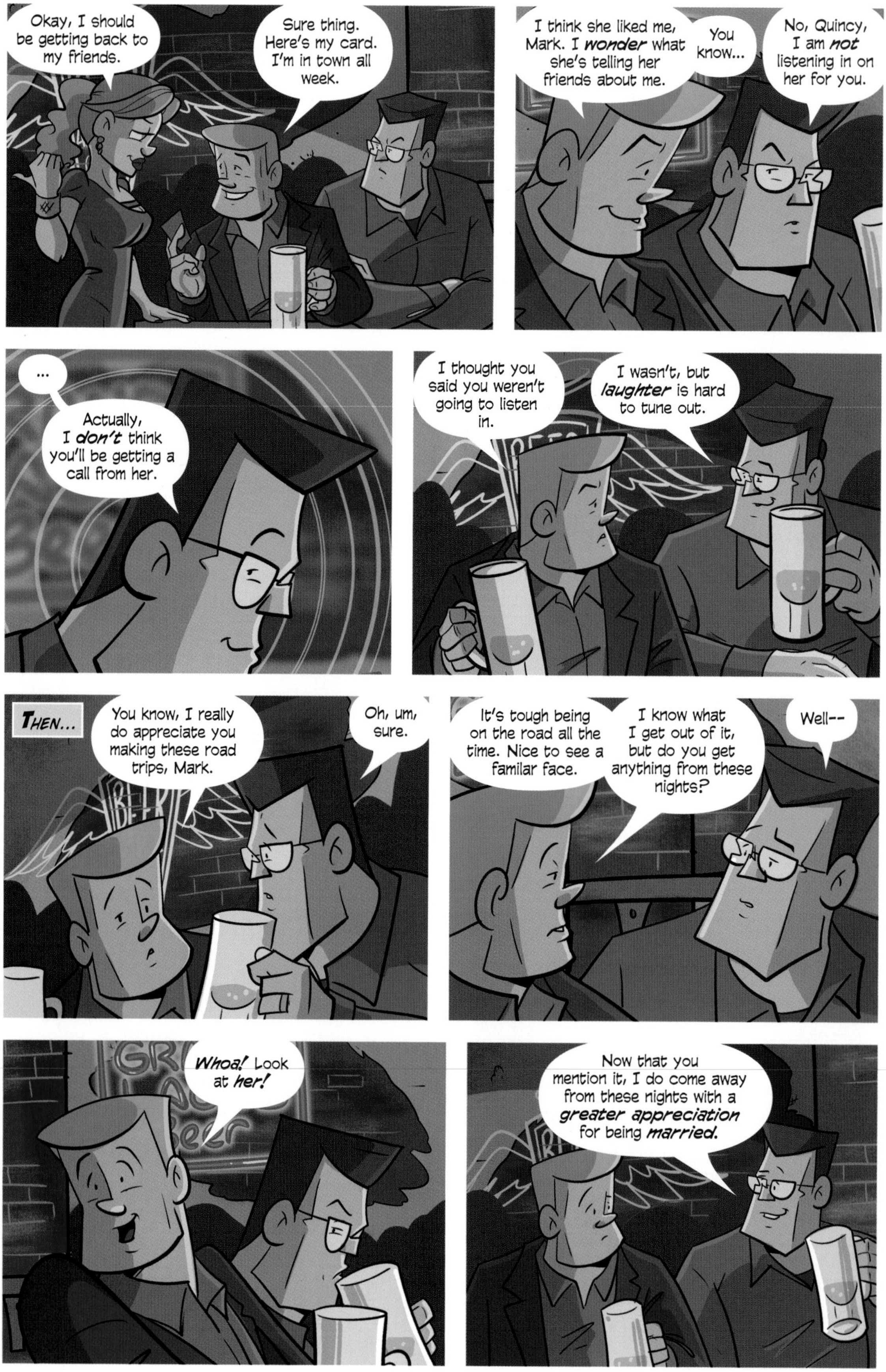
Okay, I should be getting back to my friends.
Sure thing. Here's my card. I'm in town all week.
I think she liked me, Mark. I *wonder* what she's telling her friends about me.
You know...
No, Quincy, I am ***not*** listening in on her for you.
...
Actually, I ***don't*** think you'll be getting a call from her.
I thought you said you weren't going to listen in.
I wasn't, but *laughter* is hard to tune out.
THEN...
You know, I really do appreciate you making these road trips, Mark.
Oh, um, sure.
It's tough being on the road all the time. Nice to see a familar face.
I know what I get out of it, but do you get anything from these nights?
Well--
***Whoa!*** Look at ***her!***
Now that you mention it, I do come away from these nights with a ***greater appreciation*** for being ***married.***

LATER...

Those guys have been hogging the table all night.

Somebody should take them down a peg.

You know, you being *you*, I bet we could--

Quincy, no. That's not what my gifts are for.

Yeah, I know. You're right.

They are *jerks*, though.

When I went to the bathroom, I heard them talking about how *superhero movies* aren't really *cinema*.

Okay, just this once.

FINALLY...

I think I'm calling it a night.

Sounds good.

WOO HOO!

Bridal party represent!

Tequila all around!

Hey...

Mark, I think maybe I'll stay for just one more--

Ulp! What are you doing?

Rescuing.

Who?

Everyone.

It sure is *windy* out there tonight--

--*wait.*

If you're going to *come by* to rake the leaves, don't forget to say hello to your *mother.*

**LATER...**

You know, you really *don't* need to keep taking care of the lawn for us.

But I don't mind.

You do *too much,* Mark.

I wonder where I learned that from? Maybe some *nurse* who also was a *room mother* for my class *and* ran for city council?

Still, Jane's boy down the street has a *lawn service.* We could hire him.

Wait, *Todd?*

I went to high school with him.

I'd rather you hired *Green Thumbelina* on work release. At least she'd leave you the silver.

So, how's Dad's *physical therapy* going?

He still *hates* it. Grouches about it the whole time.

But he's going.

And he's moving a *little better* every day.

Plus, I keep moving things around the house so he has to *walk more*.

Geez, that's a little Darkblade-ish, Mom.

No, that's just forty years of being a *nurse*.

AND SO...

So are we still coming out next month?

*Absolutely!* James has that Monday off for teachers in-service, so we've got a long weekend.

And *no planes* for you anymore. I'm bringing you out.

No arguments from us these days. TSA is even *less fun* when one of you has metal implants.

So, we're glad to fly Air Crusader--

--as long as we're in *first class*, of course.

Always, Mom. Love you.

Love you, too.

THAT MORNING...

Wh-- huh?

What time is it?

Mark? Did I *oversleep?* It was my turn to wake up with the kids.

Yeah, but I was *already up*, so I let you sleep.

Mom! Dad made breakfast!

Well that was very nice of him, James.

*Made* breakfast, huh?

Mark, you know the kids like it when you *actually* make breakfast, right?

Yeah, I know. I was just passing by Stuttgart on my way home.

Long night?

Yeah. After getting Quincy home, I did the *leaves* at my parents and then there was this *flood* in Poland...

Well, I know long nights come with the job, but I miss sleeping next to you.

Leave the *late nights* to Paul.

Yeah, me too.

You know, a lack of a *warm bed* and *snuggles* is probably why he's so grouchy all the time.

I have *no doubt.*

*LATER...*

I love going to the park!

Us too, James.

Crisp fall day, my family playing in the park. Sometimes our lives are straight out of the *Hallmark Channel.*

They are!

And I love the *fractal designs* that leaves make in the *air currents* as they fall.

And then sometimes they go *straight SyFy.*

Are you saying we're too old for *the CW?*

*THEN...*

Come on, Dad! *Higher!*

Higher!

Higher still?

Dad, I want you to push me as *hard* as *you can!*

As hard as I can?

No.

Just no.

AND...

Dad, look how *high* I am!

That's *great*, James! Can you see our building from there?

Mark, I *don't* like it when he's up so high.

But what if he *falls?*

Oh, he's fine.

Then I'll catch him.

Besides, we can't have him being scared of *heights.*

Fine, but *you're* the one taking him here from now on.

THEN...

Mark, *come here!*

What is it?

Hayley just *looked* at that squirrel and it *stopped.* Can she talk to the animals? Is that a thing?

I'm sure it's *not.* It's a squirrel. It just stopped for a minute.

Yeah, you're right.

Let's switch. James wants to show you how *fast* he can spin you on the merry-go-round.

That's *not* a thing, right?

MONInG MORNING...

James, **wake up!** Time to get ready for school.

Mommy, I don't feel so good.

Aw, honey, you feel hot. You might have a fever. Maybe you should **stay home** today.

But I have a **test** today. I don't want to miss that.

James, I know you take after your father, but it's nice every once in a while to know you've got some of **me** in there, too.

I think James caught that cold that's been going around.

I'm going to keep him home today.

Oh, poor guy!

How's he doing?

He's mostly upset he's missing school. This'll be his **first** sick day.

I used to love sick days.

Staying in my pajamas and watching *Price is Right, Sale of the Century, Supermarket Sweep...*

I have a feeling this will be more of a Netflix binge of *Whoa Bots*.

Streaming is **ruining** a classic rite of passage.

Based on **your** rite of passage, though, I see how you wound up an **accountant**.

LATER...

What are you making?

I'm heating up some *chicken noodle soup* for James.

Soup. I just *don't* get it.

I will *never* understand how you don't like soup.

I don't know why either, I just *don't.*

But soup is *so good!* It *warms* you up and makes you *feel good!* when you get sick.

Well, there you go. I don't get cold *or* sick.

You should leave before you're *wearing* this soup, showoff.

THEN...

Abby, I have to take off for a minute.

Okay.

You know, *"take off."*

Yeah. Consider those tea leaves *read,* Captain Subtlety.

Do we need anything while I'm out?

You know, some *ice cream* might be nice.

Oh. Is his *throat* bothering him, too?

Sure, yeah. That.

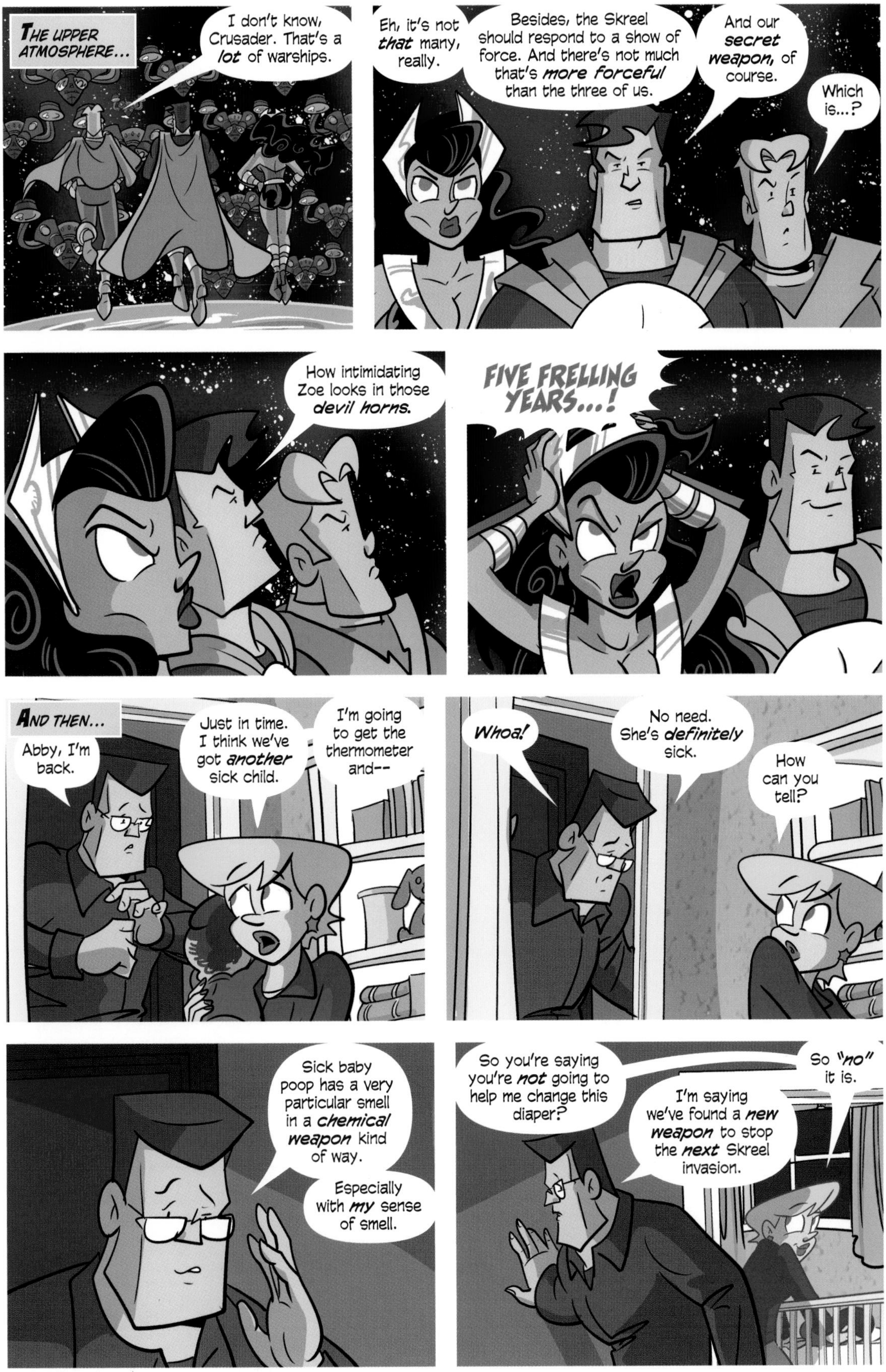
THE UPPER ATMOSPHERE...
I don't know, Crusader. That's a lot of warships.
Eh, it's not that many, really.
Besides, the Skreel should respond to a show of force. And there's not much that's more forceful than the three of us.
And our secret weapon, of course.
Which is...?
How intimidating Zoe looks in those devil horns.
FIVE FRELLING YEARS...!
AND THEN...
Abby, I'm back.
Just in time. I think we've got another sick child.
I'm going to get the thermometer and--
Whoa!
No need. She's definitely sick.
How can you tell?
Sick baby poop has a very particular smell in a chemical weapon kind of way.
Especially with my sense of smell.
So you're saying you're not going to help me change this diaper?
I'm saying we've found a new weapon to stop the next Skreel invasion.
So "no" it is.

THEN...

Abby, it's *late*. Do you want to head to bed?

They're comfortable here, and I'm sure they'll just wake up again. I'll just sleep on the couch tonight.

You don't want to *switch?*

No, it's okay. You head to bed.

This is where I gently point out that I don't actually *need* to sleep.

Good point!

My watch now is ended.

As long as it ends better than that *last episode.*

THE NEXT MORNING...

Maaark?

I think the kids' Captain Trips has claimed another victim.

Am I *hot?*

You're *always* hot to me, but I think you're running a fever.

Yeah, you're *definitely* sick.

A healthy Abby would never have let me get away with that joke.

So...

Thanks for making the *house call*, Doc.

Of course. I am but sorry I can only be here in *astral* form.

What's he saying?

Your family is but suffering from the common cold. Common, but also *quite immune* to mine magics.

It's just an ordinary cold. *Nothing* unusual.

No?

Ah... hello, little one?

Well, except that Glowbug here can *see astral projections*.

Always gonna be something with you, too, huh?

Thanks again, Doc.

It is my pleasure, Mark. I just wish I could do *more*.

You know, for everything all of us can *do*, why *haven't* we done anything like cure the common cold?

In my case, keeping the *multiverse* spinning on its axis is quite the consuming task.

That said, did not the Evil Brain once say that *he* had discovered a *cure* for it?

So what became of that restorative?

Yeah. That one time he'd *gone straight*.

Once he started dealing with the *insurance companies*, he *unreformed* and destroyed it.

Ah, yes. I do understand the call of that *dark path*.

*LATER...* Hey, Mark. Abby wanted me to bring the *mail* from the store.

Um, thanks.

Okay, so... the *hazmat suit...?*

The store can't afford *both* of us being sick. It's just common sense.

Sure. Okay, yeah.

Wait. No.

What is it?

Do I want to know *where* you got a hazmat suit?

Mrs. O'Lonergan has *really* interesting taste in housewarming presents.

*THAT EVENING...* Are you still watching "Cupid's Arrows?"

Uh-oh.

⌇Unh!⌇

Best deathtrap ever.

THEN...

And *blow*...

Good job, buddy.

ᔍSniff!ᔌ Hey, Dad, I have a question.

Sure. What is it?

I'm sick. The baby's sick. Mommy's sick. And *you're* taking care of us.

That's true.

So what happens if *you* get sick? Who takes care of *you?*

If I get sick, we have *bigger problems* than who takes care of me.

AND...

Hey, Mom.

James is doing a *little* better. Abby and Hayley shouldn't be far behind.

But yeah, it's mostly been me running my own private MASH unit here.

I'm sure you're *doing fine.* Nursing is in your blood.

And I wish I'd had *your powers* when I was at the hospital.

You *wouldn't* say that if you could see germs.

THEN...

Mark, are you doing the *laundry*, too?

Huh? Oh, yeah.

Honey, you're doing *too much.*

Don't worry about it. It's *fine.* And it's all stuff that needs to be done.

Sure but--

--um, Mark? You realize these are *my* clothes, right?

Because I don't think my blue cardigan needed to be *super compressed* to fit in your cape pouch.

*Whoops!* Sorry.

Still. Marie Kondo would *kill* to fold like this.

AND...

Abby, I can get her--

Mark, it doesn't matter how sick I am, I'll *always* have time to mom.

Besides, I think I'm on the *tail end* of this thing.

Okay. Well, is there *anything* I can do for you?

You know, now that you mention it. My *appetite* is coming back. I could use some food.

I've got a bit of a yearning for *Indian.*

Let me get some *rupees* out of the safe. Bademiya doesn't take *plastic.*

LATER...

Zashi, Charlotte. Is Abby still *sick?*

*Whole family,* I'm afraid. But she didn't want you to have to wait for this.

One *History of Liberty City,* 1912 edition.

This will be a *great gift* for the Mayor when they present me the key to the city.

So, how's life in the *sick ward?*

Pretty good. Mark's taking great care of them. Heck, I don't think he's slept *all week.*

What?

I said Mark hasn't slept all week. Is there a problem? He doesn't *need* to sleep.

No, but he does need to *rest.*

Charlotte, I have to go. Will you keep this for me?

Is this *serious?*

Nothing we can't take care of.

Oh, by the way, your new tiara looks *great.*

FIVE YEARS!

TINK!  TINK!

CHRONOPOLIS...

Amazonia? Is everything *okay* with you?

With *me*, yes. But not with *Mark*.

His family has been sick all week, so he's been taking care of them.

And *not* sleeping.

*All* week?

*Yes.* I figured *you* have a plan for this, but if not, I can--

No, I'd rather not have him in the *infirmary*.

My thought exactly.

Do you know *where* he is?

His Liberty League communicator last showed him in Southern California.

Okay, I'll call the Airblade.

Paul, it's faster if *I* take you.

...

You're right, of course.

So hold on.

I thought that was *your* job!

Crusader? How are you?

Darkblade? What brings *you* out here?

I was going to ask *you* the same thing.

I came out to deal with the *fires*.

Well, that's good.

But what about *this*?

Oh, that—?

I just thought the letters should be in *alphabetical order*.

OH LLOOWY

Right.

So, buddy, you *haven't slept* in a while. And you know how you get when you don't rest.

Yeah, but I'm *fine* this time. You don't have to worry.

We've been over this. When you don't rest, your brain doesn't *reset*. You start making questionable decisions. You're *not* capable--

I'm the most powerful man on the planet. I'm nothing *but* capable.

That kind of response doesn't fill me with *confidence*, buddy. Why don't we head home--

Why don't you *make me*?

Yeah, that's what I was *afraid* you were going to say.

75

**60 SECONDS LATER...**

Zoe, I need some *backup.*

On my way.

Darkblade, what's the problem? He's already *out.*

Well, sure.

So what did you need *me* for?

He's *heavy.*

*How* did you do that? How did you take down the Crusader in *one minute?*

Forty-five seconds.

And planning.

Mark's been worried about this scenario since it first happened *fifteen years ago.* So we *gamed out* a solution.

It only works if he's *not* in control of his faculties. If he was, I wouldn't have lasted *half* that long.

The *actual* solution is between him and me, which is why I asked you to *hang back.*

Fair.

Plus it involves him focusing on me alone, and you *do* draw attention.

I'm glad you still notice.

76

Abby?

Zoe, thanks for bringing him *home*.

Where are the kids...?

Charlotte's *upstairs* making sure they stay in their rooms.

You can just drop him in the chair.

*Paul,* it's good to see you again. It's been *too long.*

It has.

Do you need any help?

No. I'll get him changed *after* you leave. Let him keep a little bit of dignity.

At least until he sees that *YouTube video* he posted.

He does so much, you know? And he takes such good care of us.

Of *everyone,* really.

He just got a little *lost* on the way this time.

That's true.

He *warned* me about this once, but I've never actually seen him lose it.

Did he cause any huge problems?

Not really. We caught it early.

He *did* make some edits to the Hollywood sign.

Well, they're *used* to getting notes that make things worse out there.

FINALLY...

It was good **working** with you again, Paul.

Yeah. You, too.

Did you want to get some **coffee** or something?

It's been a while and--

--well, it'd be nice to **catch up**. I **miss** my friend, you know?

I--

≫Sigh!≪

Well... I don't miss **that**.

THE NEXT MORNING...

Is Daddy **sick**, Mommy?

He's mostly just **tired** from taking care of us this past week--

--so now we get to return the favor.

It's what **families** do.

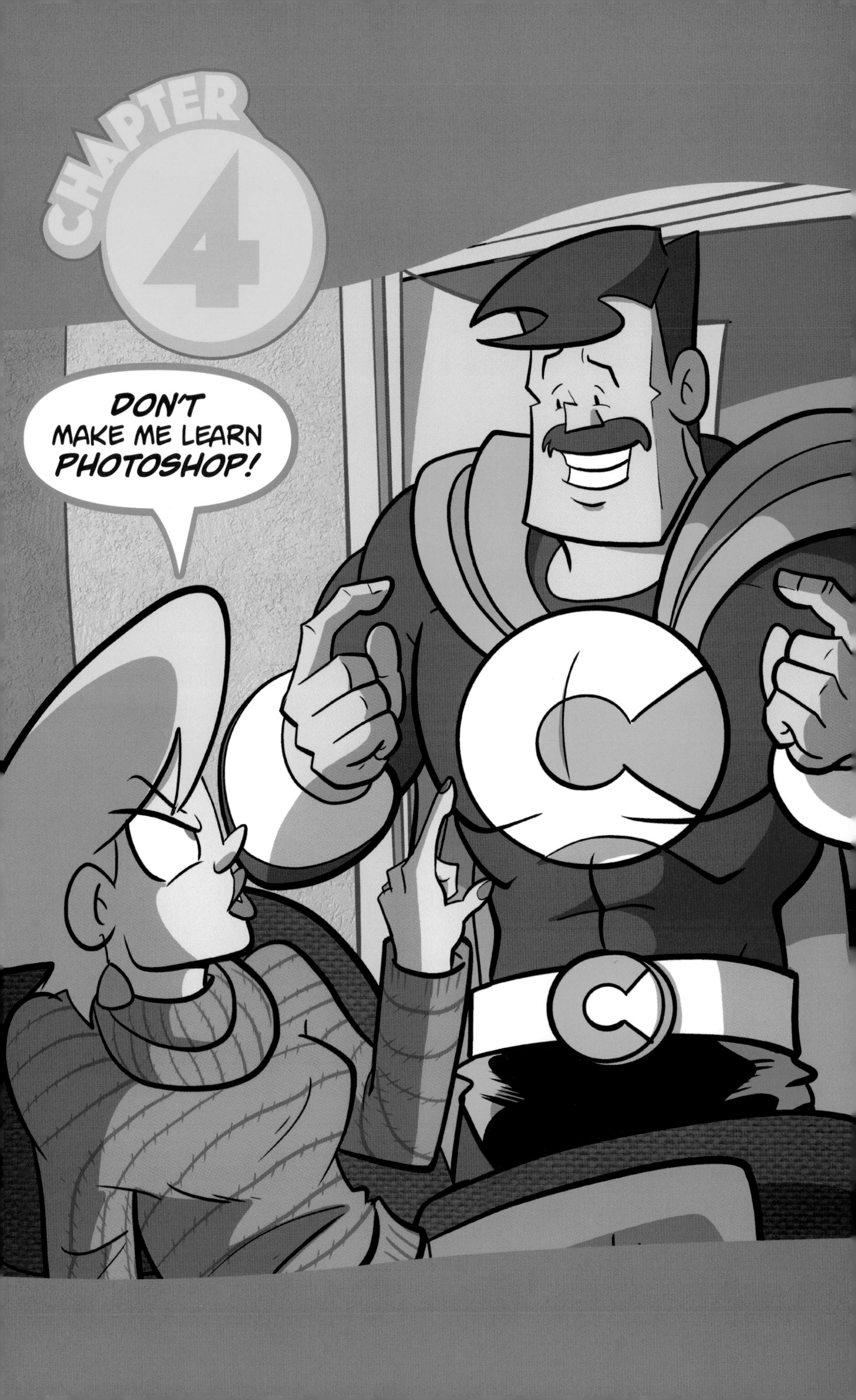
CHAPTER 4
DON'T MAKE ME LEARN PHOTOSHOP!

"WHEREVER THERE IS CRIME OR TRIVIA,
THAT'S WHERE I'LL BE."

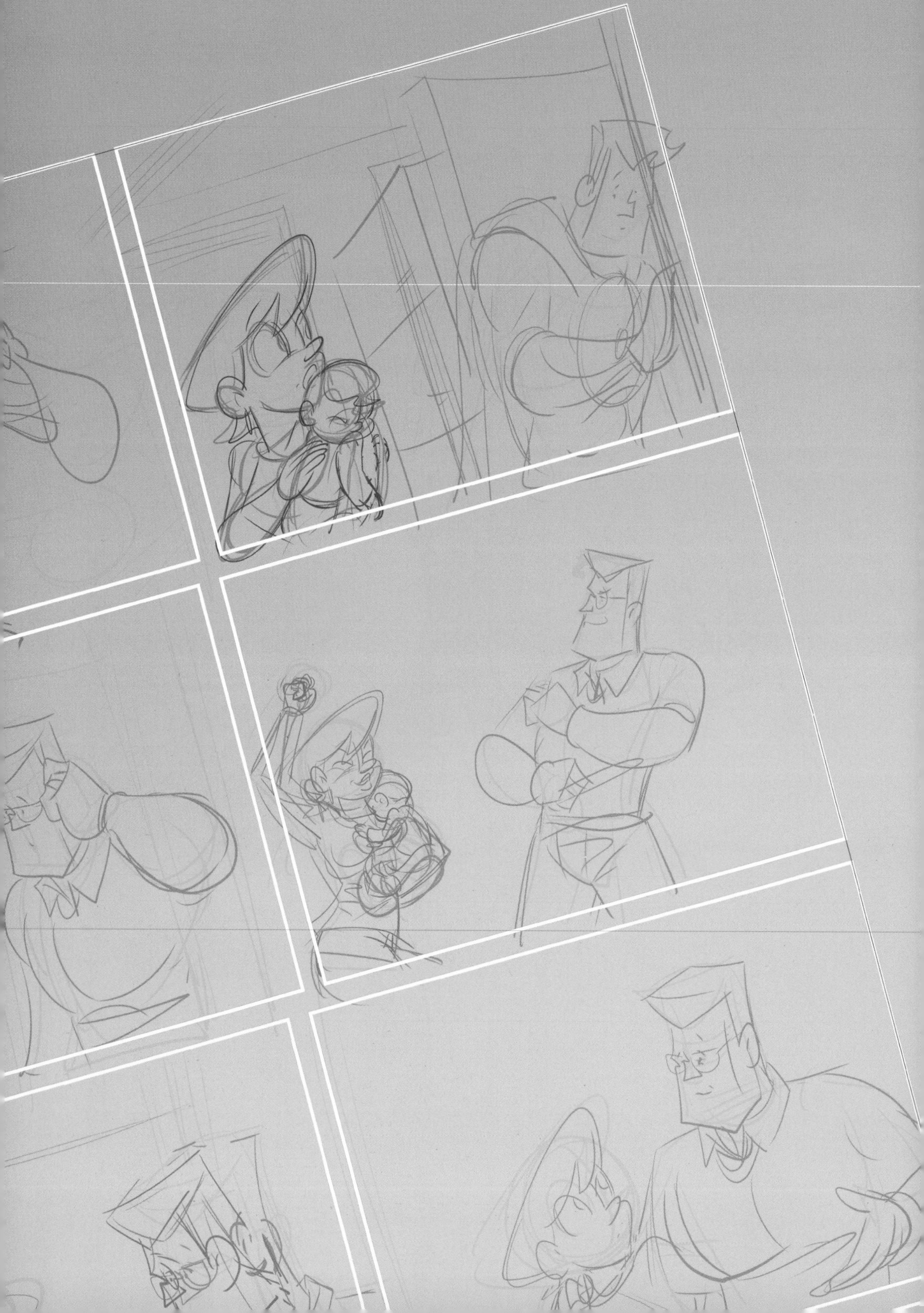

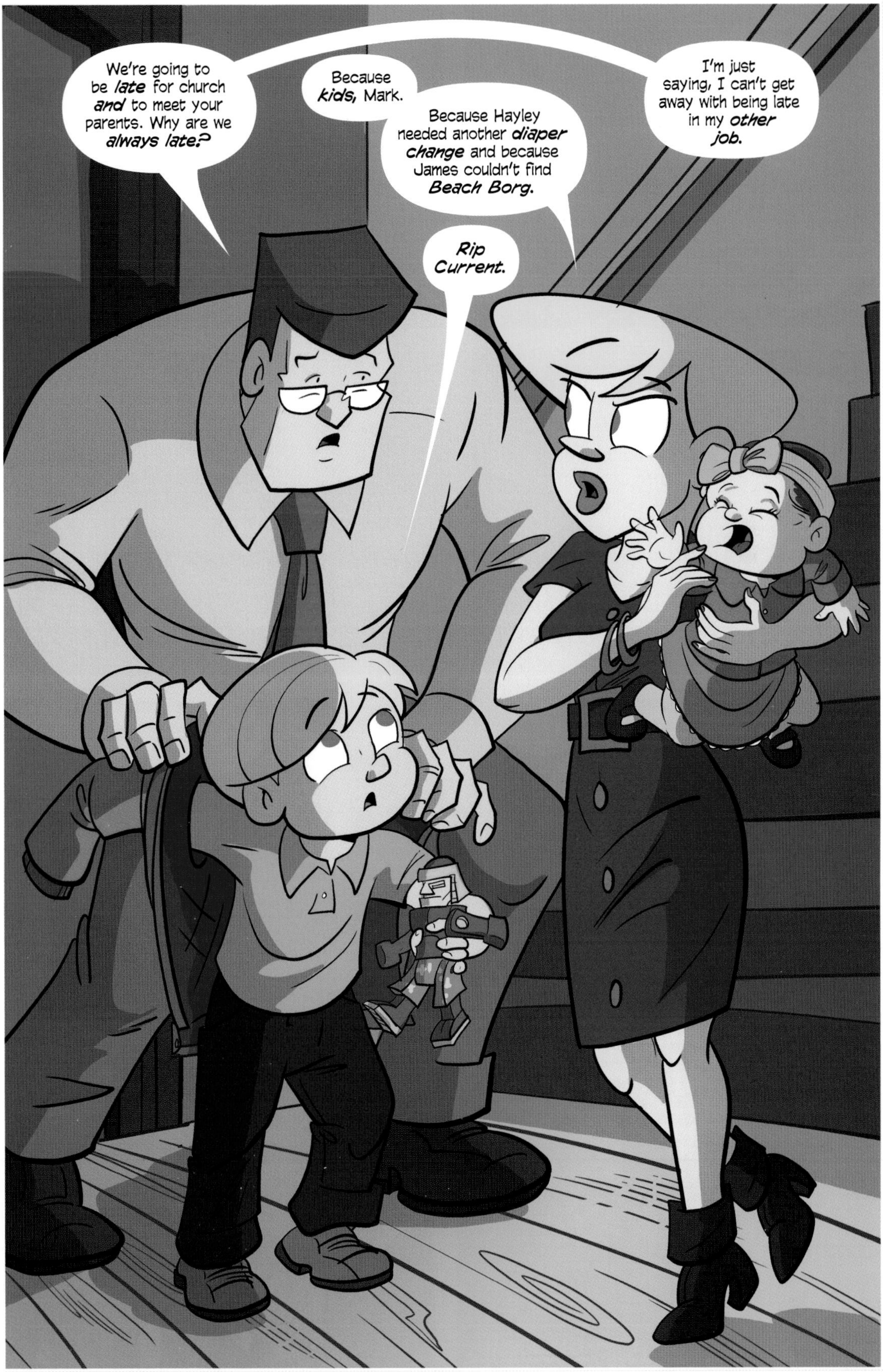
We're going to be *late* for church *and* to meet your parents. Why are we *always late?*
Because *kids,* Mark.
Because Hayley needed another *diaper change* and because James couldn't find *Beach Borg.*
*Rip Current.*
I'm just saying, I can't get away with being late in my *other job.*

Is that because you'd have to file a *sten'shin*, Dad?

Well, Mark?

*"Extension,"* James. And yes, that's it *exactly.*

Hey, would you go grab Hayley's pony for us?

Sure!

You're going to need to watch it. He's starting to hear *everything.*

And he's perceptive like his mother.

Nice save, Hero Boy.

So, are we ready to go, Hayley?

*Wait,* one more thing.

I guess we're *not.*

Can't go without her diaper bag.

Diapers, wipes, Cheerios--all the essentials. *So many* essentials.

Okay, let's head out.

You know, Paul offered to design a *diaper belt* for us.

Yeah, but it wouldn't go with anything, would it?

It'd probably be *utilitartian.*

Hey, when did you get your jacket?

I change pretty fast, remember?

THEN...

--and we're going to Flapjack Flophouse!

Ooh, I love that place. Can I come, too?

And hello there, Hayley.

Nice to see you *not* crying.

Yeah, I'm sorry about that. She just wouldn't stay quiet.

It's okay. Bring forth to me *all* the screaming children. I'll just talk louder.

Besides, I appreciate anything that keeps Miles *awake* through my homilies.

By the way, I appreciated the He-Man reference in that homily.

I had a feeling you'd catch that.

And also, nice catch with that satellite. I saw that on the news.

Thank you, Father.

Flapjack time!!

I forget sometimes that Father Jerry, ah, *knows*.

He's a good counsellor.

Sometimes even a super power needs to check in with a *higher* power.

THEN...

--we were thinking maybe a cruise.

Oh, that sounds nice.

Dad, can I have some more flapjacks? I'm *still hungry.*

Still?

You've got quite a *super* appetite, James.

Don't worry. That shouldn't actually kick in for a few years.

Good. That'll give us time to *expand* the pantry.

ONE STACK LATER...

Happy now?

How was Hayley's checkup, Abby?

She was not happy about getting a shot, but everything else was excellent.

Good.

The doctor said she's in the 75th percentile for height and weight.

And in the *Zeta Level* for future powers.

LATER...

Let's go get the coats, James.

Abby?

Yes, I--

Oh, my goodness-- *Bria!*

James, this is a friend of Mommy's from when she was in coillege.

Hello.

I was going to ask, but I think I can *see* what's new with you.

No, the *new one's* still at the table with Daddy.

*So...*

It is *so good* running into you, Bria. Are you in town long?

A couple of weeks.

Oh, she's a cutie.

Hey, why don't I go take the kids to the car?

You can catch up a bit and I'll bring the car around.

Thanks!

If Doug had been that attentive, I'd still be married.

I know I told you this at the wedding, but you got one of the *good* ones.

You have *no idea.*

85

So what brings you back into town this time?

I've got a meeting with Gracen and Gracen, so I thought I'd turn it into a visit with my parents.

I was also supposed to do a local news hit on my book, but I just got a call that they're *cancelling* that.

I *hate* missing a chance to self-promote.

Well, we can fix that. I own the bookstore over on Jefferson.

Maybe we can put together a *signing* while you're in town.

Really? That'd be *great!*

Come on by. We'll have some coffee, catch up, and plan some general hijinks.

You know, the last time we did that--

Hey, we *still graduated.*

CHRONOPOLIS...

You know what day it is, right?

Yeah. Maybe he's forgotten.

He *never* forgets.

*Crusader!* My old *playmate!*

Quizzle.

Told you.

⸘Sigh!� I know.

Remember the rules: I'll *only* return home once you successfully answer my trivia question.

This one's a toughie. How many appearances did *Colonel Flagg* have on M*A*S*H?

Counting "Deal Me Out?" Seven.

Oh, flerk.

One of these days, he's going to figure out that I'm feeding you the answers.

He never said I couldn't *phone a friend.*

POP!

86

It's disappointingly *quiet* tonight.

Less crime is always a *good* thing.

Hey, I saw something I wanted to ask you about--

--did you sell *LaCroix Films* to *MausHaus?*

I did. They made a *good* offer.

But you had my film rights. I don't want them doing the animated *Crusader on Ice.*

Or worse yet *Liberty League Babies.*

No, they were talking feature film. Maybe a Liberty League cinematic universe.

*Don't push it.*

And a theme park ride?

So, why did you *sell* the studio? Your dad started that, and I know you enjoyed running it.

Yeah, but I've been an *absentee studio head* these days. I figured it was better to sell it to someone who would do something good with it.

Meanwhile, I can do more good elsewhere.

Okay. As long as you're sure.

You're just sorry I won't be able to get you *movie screeners* anymore.

We've got *two kids!* Do you know how hard it is to have a night out?

Heading home already?

Yeah, I think so. Nothing happening here and--

Oops! Spoke too soon!

Crusader, you were wrong! Flagg was also in *"Trials"!*

That was *AfterM\*A\*S\*H.* You only said *M\*A\*S\*H.*

See, I know things, too.

Never doubted it.

*POOF!*

So tomorrow night?

Wherever there is crime or trivia, that's where I'll be.

THE NEXT DAY...

So Bria? From college?

Art Books & Coffee

Didn't you two go on Spring Break together?

We don't talk about Spring Break.

Okay, we need a copy of *Artists at Altitude,* too.

Got it.

Yeah, it's amazing how far she's come. I mean, she ran a Fortune 500 company.

It's hard to believe were in business classes together.

Didn't you two also get arrested together?

We. Don't. Talk. About. Spring. Break.

SHORTLY...

Hey, there she is!

Abby, is this an okay time?

I'm the boss here. It's an okay time whenever I *say* it is.

Oh, good!

Coffee?

Please.

You still take it black?

Unless you've got some *Bailey's* under the cabinet.

Come back at closing time and I'll set you up.

Please tell me this place becomes a *speakeasy* at night.

Wow! You just breathe good business ideas, don't you?

THEN...

I *love* the shop, Abby!

Thanks! All those classes with Professor Quinn really paid off.

I wonder whatever happened to him.

He and his weird bolo ties are retired and living in Cork Harbour. He fishes *everyday*.

He got in touch with me after I mentioned him in that *Forbes* profile they did.

He's retired and found his own version of Heaven.

I was hoping to see him the last time I was in Ireland, but I wound up having to speak at a conference in Dublin instead.

I'll be back across the pond in October, though. Hopefully I can squeeze in a visit then.

Did you ever make it over to Ireland? I know you always *wanted* to go.

Mark and I went over a couple of times.

We don't travel as much anymore--

--but before kids we *flew all over*.

89

THEN...

--yeah, so after my time at Ding, I was brought in to run marketing at O-Tech.

I think I saw that somewhere.

Yeah, I was their first female VP. It got some coverage.

The President saw it, too. That's how I wound up on that South Korean trade delegation.

Corporate intrigue, jet setting, hobnobbing. So *glamourous.*

It's a lot of hotel rooms and sitting on airplanes, mostly.

Yeah, but you're flying *first class.* Probably meeting all sorts of people.

Says the person who had Amazonia *and* Paul LaCroix at her wedding.

Yeah, I can't say my life's not been interesting, too.

AND SO...

--I'll have my publisher send over some books.

And I'll contact the Chamber and start promoting it.

Thanks for doing this, Abby, I appreciate it. A little *local buzz* is going to help with my meeting, too.

You're helping *me* out. Besides, Wildcats forever, right?

Wildcats forever.

See you next week!

Next week!

How you doing?

I'm happy and *not* at *all* jealous.

Totally unrelated, I told *Zoe* she might want to stop by.

You're the best.

90

Hey there. And what are you staring at with the intensity of a super villain?

I'm just hate scrolling my friend's Bria's Instagram feed.

How many Coral Reef dives can you do?

Fortunately, for you, I am well familar with the green-eyed monster.

You know, when you got together with Mark, I checked up on you, too.

Really? I--

--wait a second. Social media wasn't a thing when I started dating Mark.

I know a lot of people at the FBI, Abby.

Abby, I've spent a good chunk of my life being jealous.

First of my sisters, then of you. And what I learned is it's really not worth it.

Plus, I don't know what you have to be jealous of.

Even leaving aside Mark and the kids, you've had super powers, gone back in time, and even, unlike me lately, experienced the glory of Leandia.

Zoe, I know I've got a great life.

I just sometimes wish I could tell more people.

I know I shouldn't, but it's hard *not* to compare. She and I are the same age, went to the same school--

--and while she's one of *Business Week's* Executives to Watch, I run a, at best, moderately successful bookstore and gallery.

Why am *I* not running a Fortune 500 company?

I'd offer to make you CEO of the Fortune 500 company I just bought, but I know you *wouldn't* want that.

Let's not be too hasty.

*Which* company?

Thanks for coming by to talk. I'm sure you had *more important* things to take care of.

*Friends* are important.

You *are* a good friend, Zoe.

Yeah, I knew it.

You were being so sweet I just couldn't say anything.

THEN...

Hey there, you two!

Hayley! Mommy's home!

How are things around here?

Well, it's been a little stressful. I don't know if you saw, but there're a lot of sunspots today.

So it's messing up the cable? The WiFi?

Not exactly.

Ah.

AND...

Oh, there's my friend Glowbug!

Good news! Steel Worker has a neutrino shield we can borrow. I'll grab it after we put her down.

So how was your day?

Well, I spent the day in the shadow of my tremendously successful college friend feeling *completely insignificant.*

But my *superhero warrior princess friend* came by to make me feel better.

I know I shouldn't be, but there may be a little envy bubbling up.

That's unders--

You know, maybe I'll leave now.

Good idea.

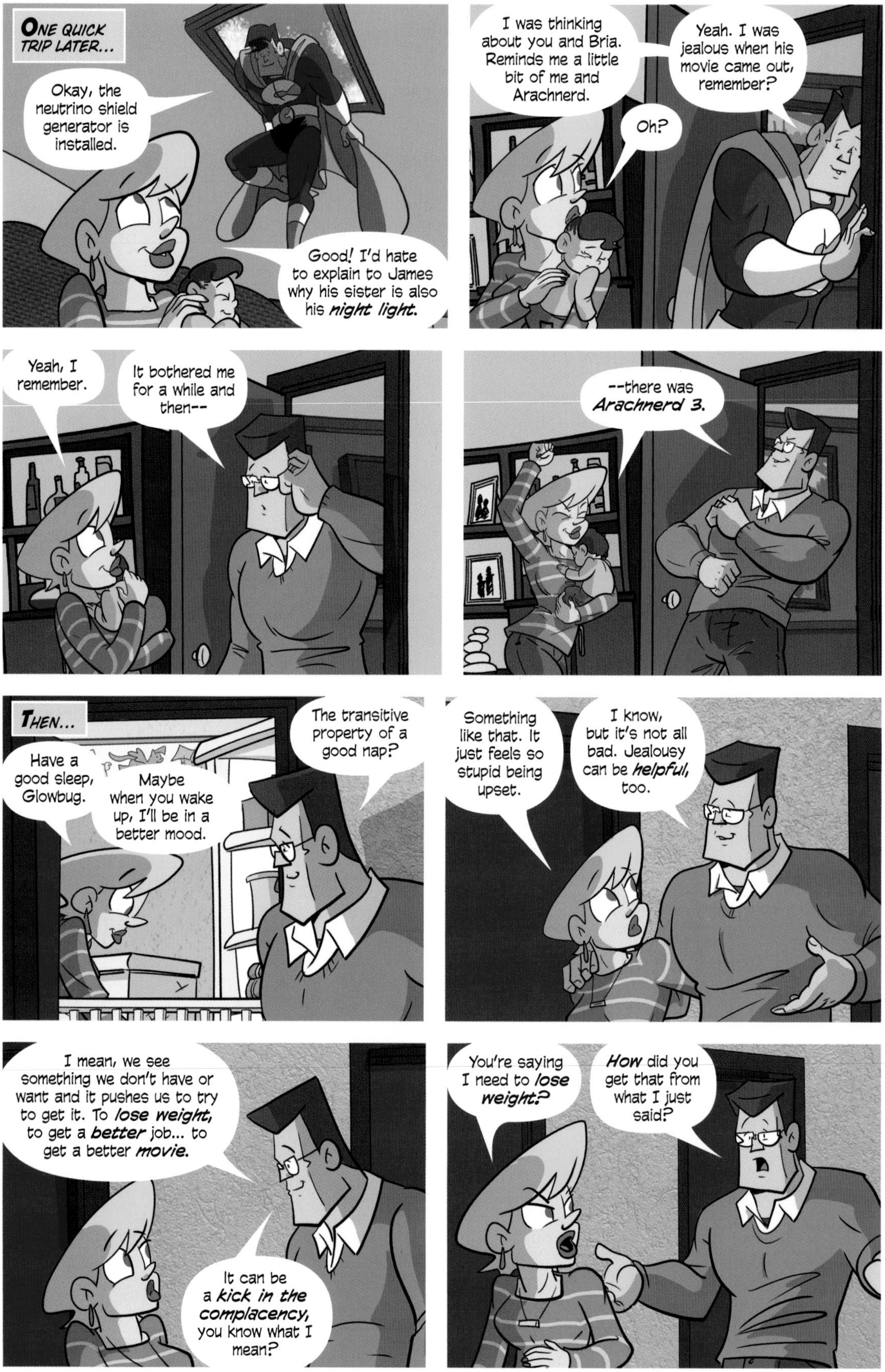

ONE QUICK TRIP LATER...
Okay, the neutrino shield generator is installed.
Good! I'd hate to explain to James why his sister is also his *night light.*
I was thinking about you and Bria. Reminds me a little bit of me and Arachnerd.
Oh?
Yeah. I was jealous when his movie came out, remember?
Yeah, I remember.
It bothered me for a while and then--
--there was *Arachnerd 3.*
THEN...
Have a good sleep, Glowbug.
Maybe when you wake up, I'll be in a better mood.
The transitive property of a good nap?
Something like that. It just feels so stupid being upset.
I know, but it's not all bad. Jealousy can be *helpful,* too.
I mean, we see something we don't have or want and it pushes us to try to get it. To *lose weight,* to get a *better* job... to get a better *movie.*
It can be a *kick in the complacency,* you know what I mean?
You're saying I need to *lose weight?*
*How* did you get that from what I just said?

**LATER...**

That was Eva. She says James is on his way up.

I'm glad James has a friend *in* the *building.* And I really like *Toby.*

Me, too.

James!

Mom! Dad! I had *so much fun* at Toby's!

What did you do, buddy?

Toby went to *MausPark!* He got all this cool stuff to play with! Dad, can *we* go to MausPark? It looks *so fun!*

I want to go to MausPark so *so* much!

Um, sometime I'm sure.

I *hate* Toby.

**AND THEN...**

Oh, hey, they have *Darkblade Adventures!*

Let's try that.

MAUS HAUZ *plus*

I EMPATHIZE WITH MARTIN    DARKBLADE ADVENTURES    UNDERFOOT, THE

What made you decide to get the *MausHaus Plus* service?

There was a deal online. Besides, the kids *love* their movies. I know we'll use it.

Your video will start in one minute. But first--

--a behind the scenes look at the magic of MausPark...

*MausPark!!*

They're *evil geniuses.*

Forget that! I need a streaming service!

Shhhh...!

THEN...

--and MausPark has the *Defenders of the Future* ride, too.

It does sound like a wonderful place.

Maybe we'll go sometime.

He's going to dream dreams of MausPark, I'm sure.

The streaming service has reached his brain.

Hey, you know what? The kids are *down* and we have the rest of the night to *ourselves*.

So...

Yes?

I was just thinking there's something we haven't done in a while.

Yes?

*Plan a trip!*

We haven't done a *research night* in forever!

I am a lucky man.

Oooh! And we can use the *new binders* I bought last month!

LATER...

Whoa, MausPark is *not* cheap.

No. It'll be a *huge trip.* But I think it'll be worth it. The kids will *love* it.

You can get lunch with some of the characters. How cool is that and--

--oh! They've got a *Brews and Booze Festival,* too. Mommy could totally go for that.

Four plane tickets to Florida are more than my first *car.*

Yeah, but that was a beat up *Fiero.* Not really a *high bar* there.

Flying is *so boring,* too.

We could always *drive.* Make it a family road trip.

*Driving?* That's even worse. Can't we just tell James who I am?

FERRO CITY...

Hey, Steel Worker. I'm returning your neutrino shield.

I hope it helped.

So much. Thank you again.

My pleasure.

What are you working on?

Your friend the Evil Brain has an *insidious new plot*. I'm building the *solution*.

So what is it?

A one dollar *universal phone cable adapter*.

Let's see him try to profit from designing a *new Apple connector* now.

THEN...

Crusader, I could have had one of the Waldoes do that.

You *always* return another man's tools.

You want to stay for a *beer?* I just bought a case of Great Lakes' new microbrew...

Sounds good.

Wait, it's not an IPA, is it?

Nope. It's a sour--

Hold that thought. I know I'm not from around here, but--

--*giant particle beams* are not normal here, are they?

They are *not*.

Come on. Let's get our hands dirty.

Tremble, Ferro City! *Tremble* before the might of--

--*Atomic Piledriver!*

That's far enough, Piledriver!

The Girdered Guardian! Did you think I wouldn't expect you?

Yes, but were you expecting *me*, too?

¿Ulp!¿ Nope. I straight-up *was not*.

I *hate* crossovers.

*Then...*

Just hold it there another minute.

Didn't plan on helping me weld a bridge today, did you?

Didn't plan on Piledriver attacking and blowing a hole in one either.

But hey, we're super heroes. *We fix things.*

Yes, we do.

There we go. It's not pretty, but it's good enough for *goverment work.*

Literally.

Wait, your fixes *pass* the Corps of Engineers inspections?

They *never* clear mine. What's your *trick?*

Mostly it's the *Stanford engineering degree.*

A WEEK LATER...

So, are you going to be *okay* with Bria signing today?

Yeah, it'll be fine. She's perfectly pleasant about everything, it's just all *my* baggage.

So I'm going to rely on that particular set of skills that Mark has taught me from guarding his secret for so many years.

I'm gonna *fake it.*

Hey! You're *early.* I haven't gotten your coffee ready yet.

Sorry. I was always taught *ten minutes early* is *on time.*

But, I do need to call my *lawyer.* Do you have somewhere I can make that call?

Absolutely, Bria. Just go through that door that in the back to the break room.

And thanks again for doing this!

Flawless.

She probably has to buy some giant company and *shut it down,* putting hundreds out of work.

Charlotte, it's okay. Really.

Fine. But if you can't take it, let me know and I'll *take her down.*

Yeah. Right.

I'm serious--

--I'd mention that I'm going to see the new Robyn Parrish movie... since Bria's *ex* is dating her now. Get in her head a bit.

Then I'll ask if she knows Indra Nooyi, pretending not to know she beat Bria out for the *Pepsi job.*

Then, when her confidence is at her lowest, show her pictures of your kids to remind her she's going to *die alone.*

You picked your skills up from Mark--

--I got mine from *Paul.*

Okay, I'm going to check on her, make sure she's set up. Would you get her coffee?

Without, please.

*With* or *without* iocaine powder?

Bria--?

--what the hell, Harvey? That's *not* what we talked about! We said *senior executive* VP. *Not* group.

I'm not coming in to be some *figurehead* to help them through a PR storm. I'm trying to build something here.

And that means being *one chair* away from the big one.

No, you tell Jim that if hes going to pull that, my next call will be to Pete--

EMPLO
ONLY

*Shortly...*

Hey, you okay? I didn't mean to overhear, but that sounded *intense.*

*Corporate politics.* It's awesome.

Are you *okay?* Do you need to talk?

No. Yeah. I don't know. It's...

Look, I *love* what I do. I'm *good* at it. And I've had some remarkable opportunities--

--but there's nothing that's ever really *satisfied* me. Not for long.

I want the *thing that does*, and I think this position could be it. Or the start of it.

Do you know what I mean?

I do.

Because I found mine.

Sorry I'm late. Dinner with Bria ran a little long.

I'm sure you had a lot to talk about.

How are *you* doing?

I'm fine. But I could use a hug.

Always.

The kids are asleep and the world seems quiet. Want to tell me about your day?

I'd love to, because my emotional maelstrom has settled. I had a *great day.*

What happened?

It started when Bria had a *bad day.*

Ah. The high road.

I saw *her struggle.* She's done *so* much, but even so, she's still looking for the thing, or things, that make her feel complete.

I remember feeling like that. And *then* I opened the bookstore.

It's not the biggest or the greatest, but it is so *very perfectly mine* and what I want it to be.

And it brought Charlotte and me *closer.* It's why I met you... and why I was *ready* to meet you.

Now look at what I have: *my own* business. A great and *healthy* family. Two *wonderful* kids and a pretty okay husband.

That's great but--

--"*pretty okay?*"

Truthfully, I have an *amazing husband*... who sometimes needs help keeping his *ego* in check.

You *do* ground me.

And, like you said, *some* comparison isn't *bad*. It'll help keep me from becoming complacent.

Maybe there are some *new things* to try. New places to go.

But, even so, if this *is it*--this is a *good* it.

This is where I want to be. I am *satisfied*...

...I am *happy*.

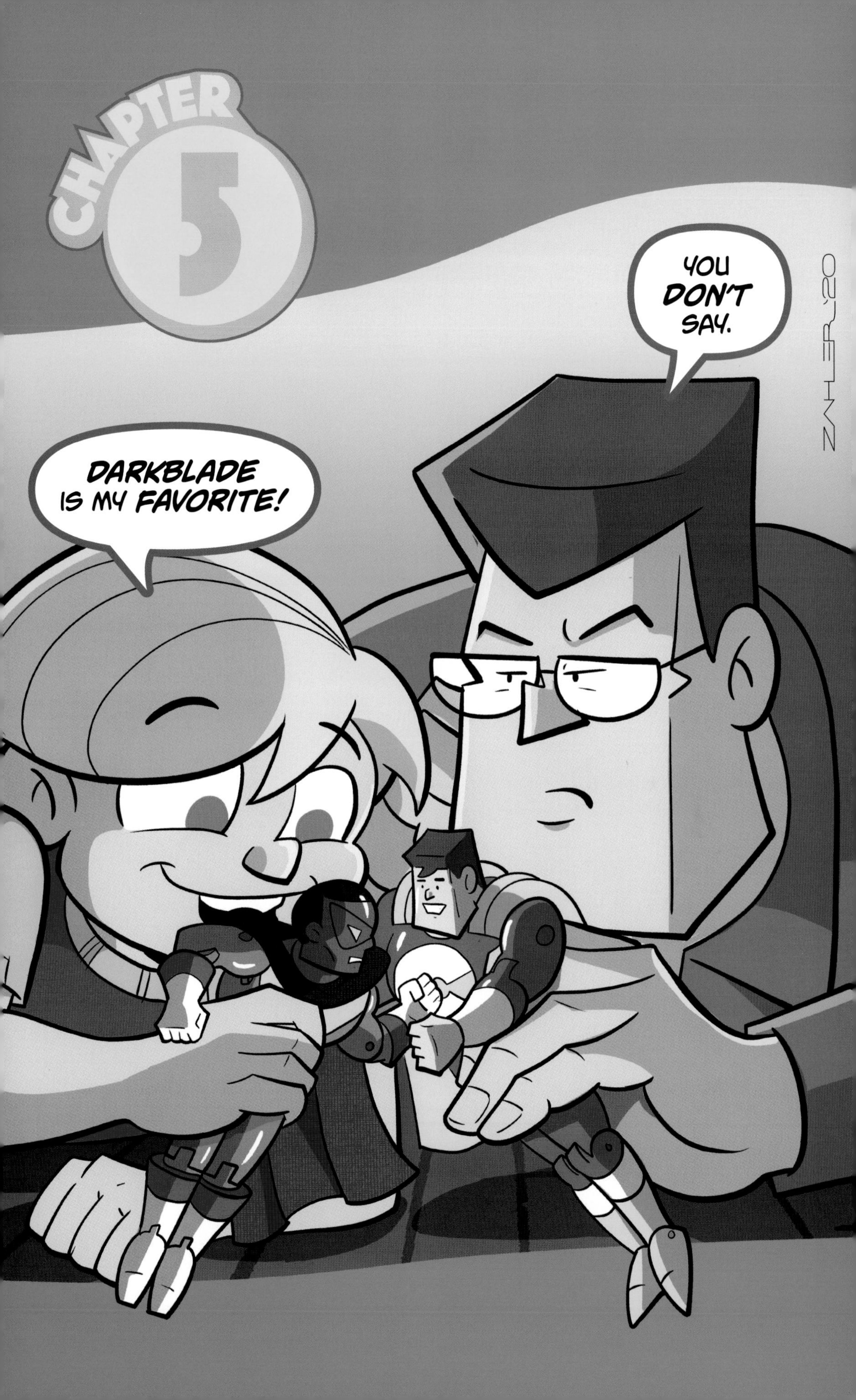
CHAPTER 5
DARKBLADE IS MY FAVORITE!
YOU DON'T SAY.

"I SEE WHY MARK MISSES THAT SKYLIGHT SO MUCH."

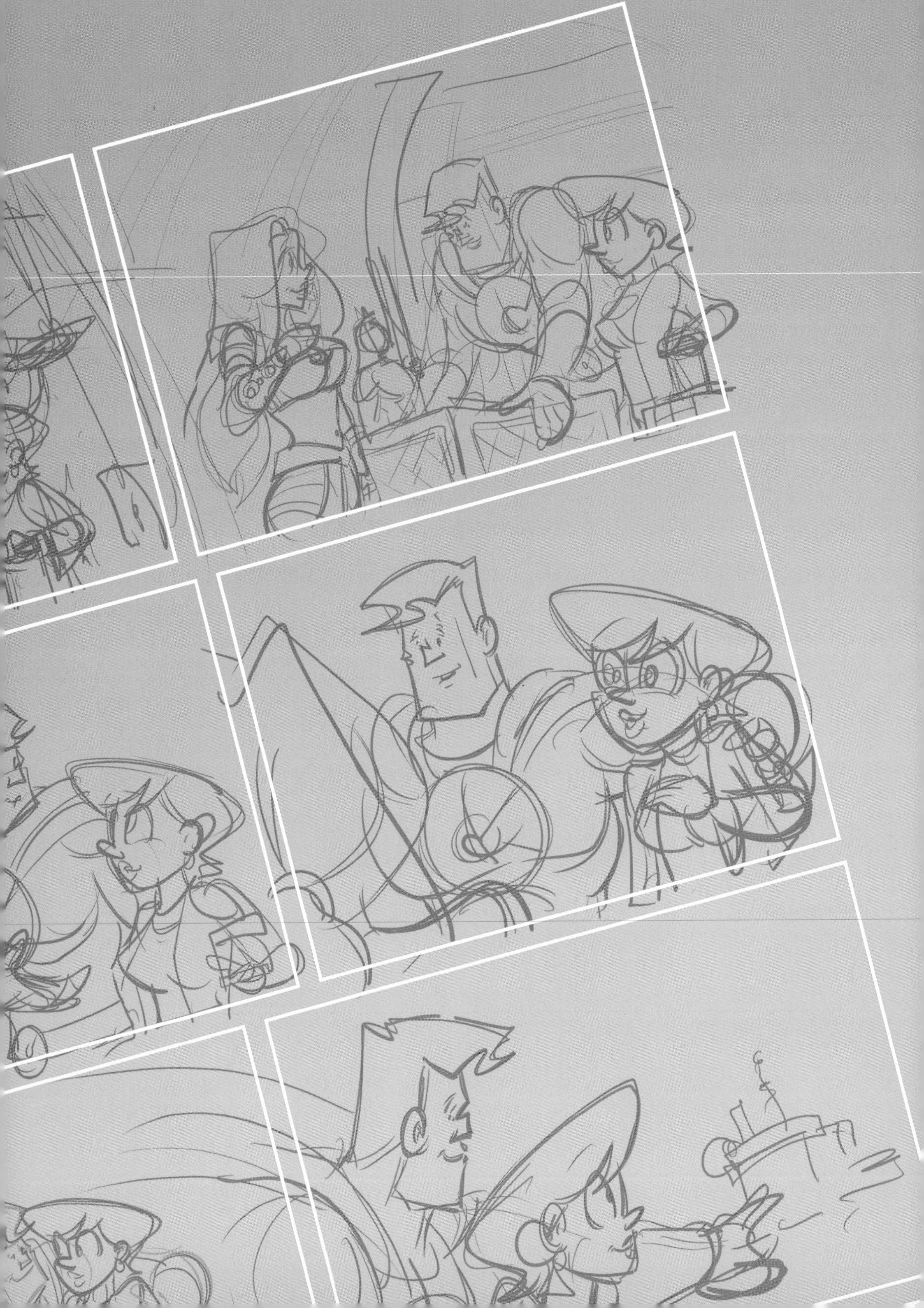

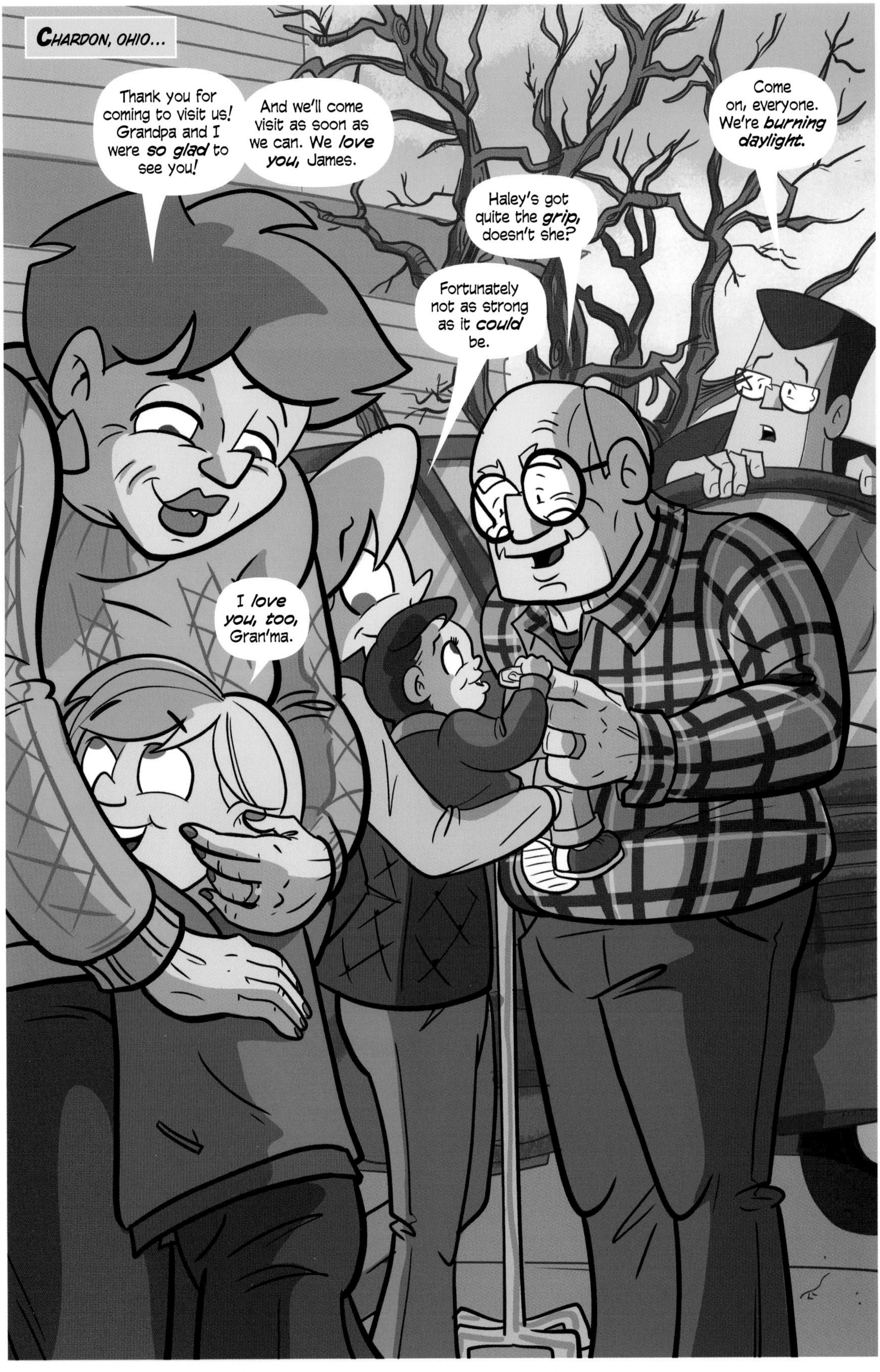

CHARDON, OHIO...
Thank you for coming to visit us! Grandpa and I were so glad to see you!
And we'll come visit as soon as we can. We love you, James.
I love you, too, Gran'ma.
Fortunately not as strong as it could be.
Haley's got quite the grip, doesn't she?
Come on, everyone. We're burning daylight.

"Burning daylight"? Congratulations on finally turning into *me*, son.

Thanks for the bag of treats, Gran'ma!

Yeah, thanks for that, Mom.

He's a growing boy. Or he *will be*.

Don't forget, I remember what it took to *fuel* you.

Well, that's true.

All right. We have to go.
I love you both. *So much*.

And be sure to call us when you get home.

We love *you* all, too.

Really? It'll probably be *late*.

Yes. We do worry.

Even about *you*.

Good-bye! Drive safe!

I think I miss them already.

Jo, do you still have the number of my *physical therapist?*

Of course. Why? Are you finally *going back?*

James asked me to play *catch* with him, and I couldn't do it with this stupid cane.

It's time to stop lollygagging and finally get better.

I want to play catch with my grandson.

And when he starts throwing like his father?

All the more reason to get my catches in while I can.

INTERSTATE 80...

Dad, can I turn on my screen and watch WhoaBots?

Yes, James. We're on a long enough trip.

Are you going to be *okay* driving?

Yeah, it's just... for me driving is like that antique car ride at the amusement park--

--when you're an *adult*.

Well, I'm sorry. Is there anything I can do?

Oh! Do you still have the kids' *cold medicine?*

Yeah, but James is over his cold so--

Mark, we are *not* drugging the kids so you can zip us home.

Just an idea.

LATER...

What's *this* bozo doing?

Right now he's thanking his lucky stars that I don't have *heat vision*.

I know this is torture for you. I could *drive* if you want. You could sleep...

I appreciate it, but with my senses I'm *too sensitive* to every little move.

Don't worry. It'll be *fine*. Really.

Oh, look. *Snow.*

—well, she's still very much JoAnn, but having grandkids has *softened* her a bit.

Softened? I'd pay cash money to see that.

So what's up next for you?

Hopefully *nothing*. It feels like between the holidays and travel that we've just been in constant motion.

The perpetual treadmill.

It's *wonderful* spending time with family and friends and doing things. But it's also exhausting.

Honestly, I just need a *vacation*. Just me. And Mark.

I'm just saying, Momma's got some needs.

It's hard enough balancing Mark's work schedule with *my* work schedule and his *other* work schedule.

Yeah, you two could *really* use a weekend alone.

Hey! Why don't you *take* one?

I could call my sister and arrange for you to stay in one of our *royal beach houses*. An interdimensional AirBNB.

Really?

Absolutely. And all I ask is that you take a shipment to my sisters for me. I'm still *banished*, but *you* can go.

Well, thanks, Zoe. That actually solves my problem.

Hey, we're super heroes. We fix things.

Abby, you told me to come get you when that Bokausek shipment came in.

Charlotte! We were *just about* to talk about you.

Uh-oh. This *never* goes well for me.

Zoe offered Mark and I her vacation home for a weekend away.

But we need *someone* to watch the kids.

And you thought "Oh, Charlotte is just sitting around with *nothing* to do. She can babysit my rugrats."

Char, I--

No worries. It's *true*. I haven't been on a date in so long I'm caught up on *all* my TV shows. Besides, I *love* those rugrats.

As a fellow member of the Dry Spell Debutantes, why don't *I* come help you watch them, too?

I owe you both *so much* wine.

Uh-oh, the *three* of you? This can't be good.

You couldn't be *more wrong.*

Zoe offered us a weekend in Leandia away from the kids and—

Done.

Wait. You don't want to hear the details?

Why? You've already worked them all out, right?

Um, actually, *yes*. I did.

See, that's what I love about you. Now, let's get to packing.

So what *are* they wearing in Leandia this time of year?

It's Leandia. As *little* as possible.

**So...** --your mom and I are going to *go away* for the weekend. And your Aunt Charlotte and Miss Zoe are going to watch you and Hayley.

Oh, boy! That'll be fun! I love Aunt Charlotte!

So you're okay with this?

When Toby's parents went to Hawaii, they brought him *souvenirs*. Are you going to bring us souvenirs?

*Absolutely* we'll bring you a souvenir, James.

Also, you'll probably *win* show and tell next week.

**Then...** Mint Condition or Koo Koo Kookie Dough?

Mint Condition, please.

Now, we're going to expect you to to *help* Charlotte and Zoe with your sister, you know.

And you'll need to be on your *best* behavior. Can you do that?

Sure, Dad. I like Miss Zoe!

Aunt Charlotte says you used to date Miss Zoe *before* you married Mom.

I see I'm going to have to give your aunt some instructions, too.

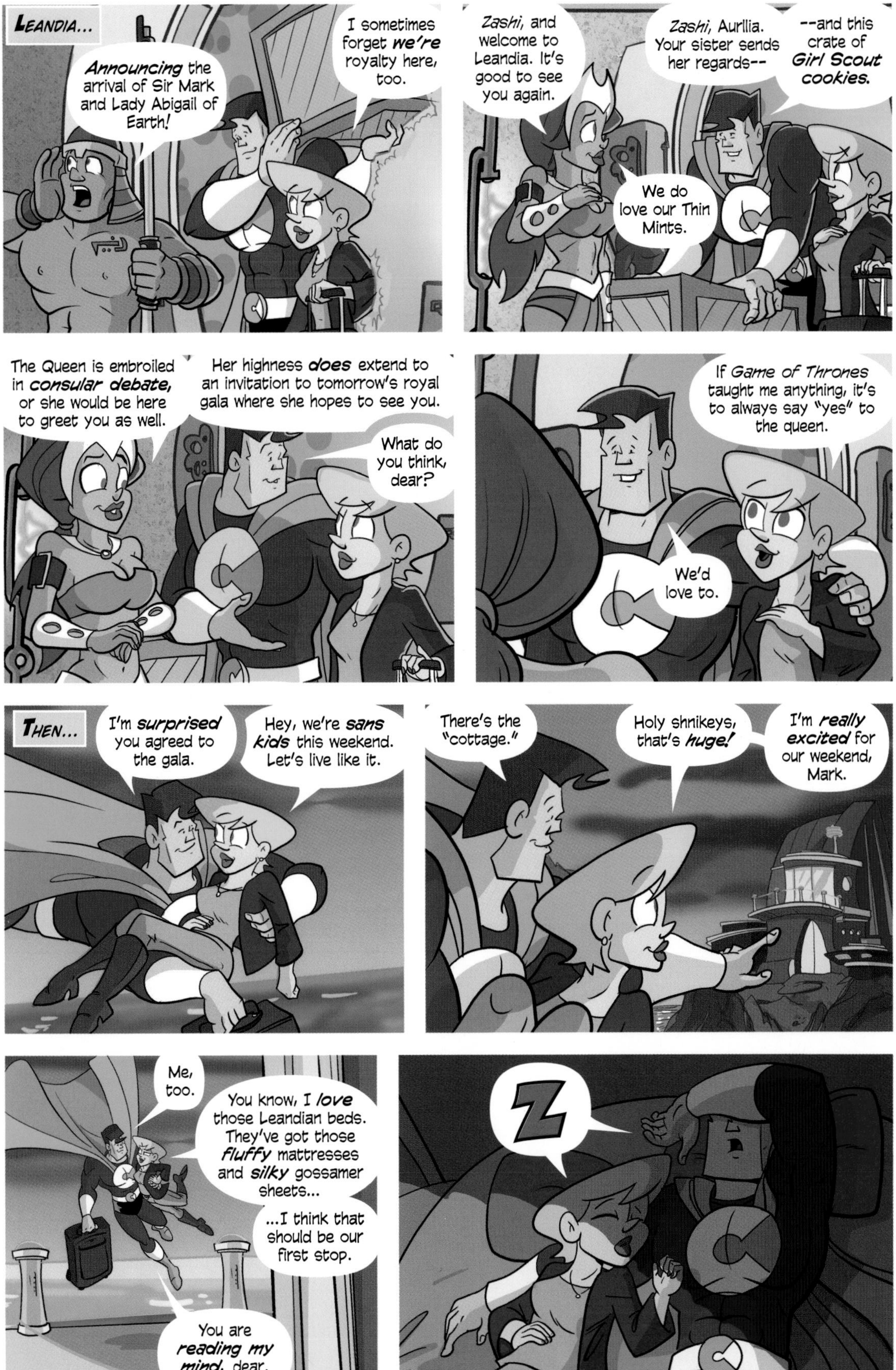
LEANDIA...
Announcing the arrival of Sir Mark and Lady Abigail of Earth!
I sometimes forget we're royalty here, too.
Zashi, and welcome to Leandia. It's good to see you again.
Zashi, Aurllia. Your sister sends her regards--
--and this crate of Girl Scout cookies.
We do love our Thin Mints.
The Queen is embroiled in consular debate, or she would be here to greet you as well.
Her highness does extend to an invitation to tomorrow's royal gala where she hopes to see you.
What do you think, dear?
If Game of Thrones taught me anything, it's to always say "yes" to the queen.
We'd love to.
THEN...
I'm surprised you agreed to the gala.
Hey, we're sans kids this weekend. Let's live like it.
There's the "cottage."
Holy shnikeys, that's huge!
I'm really excited for our weekend, Mark.
Me, too.
You know, I love those Leandian beds. They've got those fluffy mattresses and silky gossamer sheets...
...I think that should be our first stop.
You are reading my mind, dear.
Z

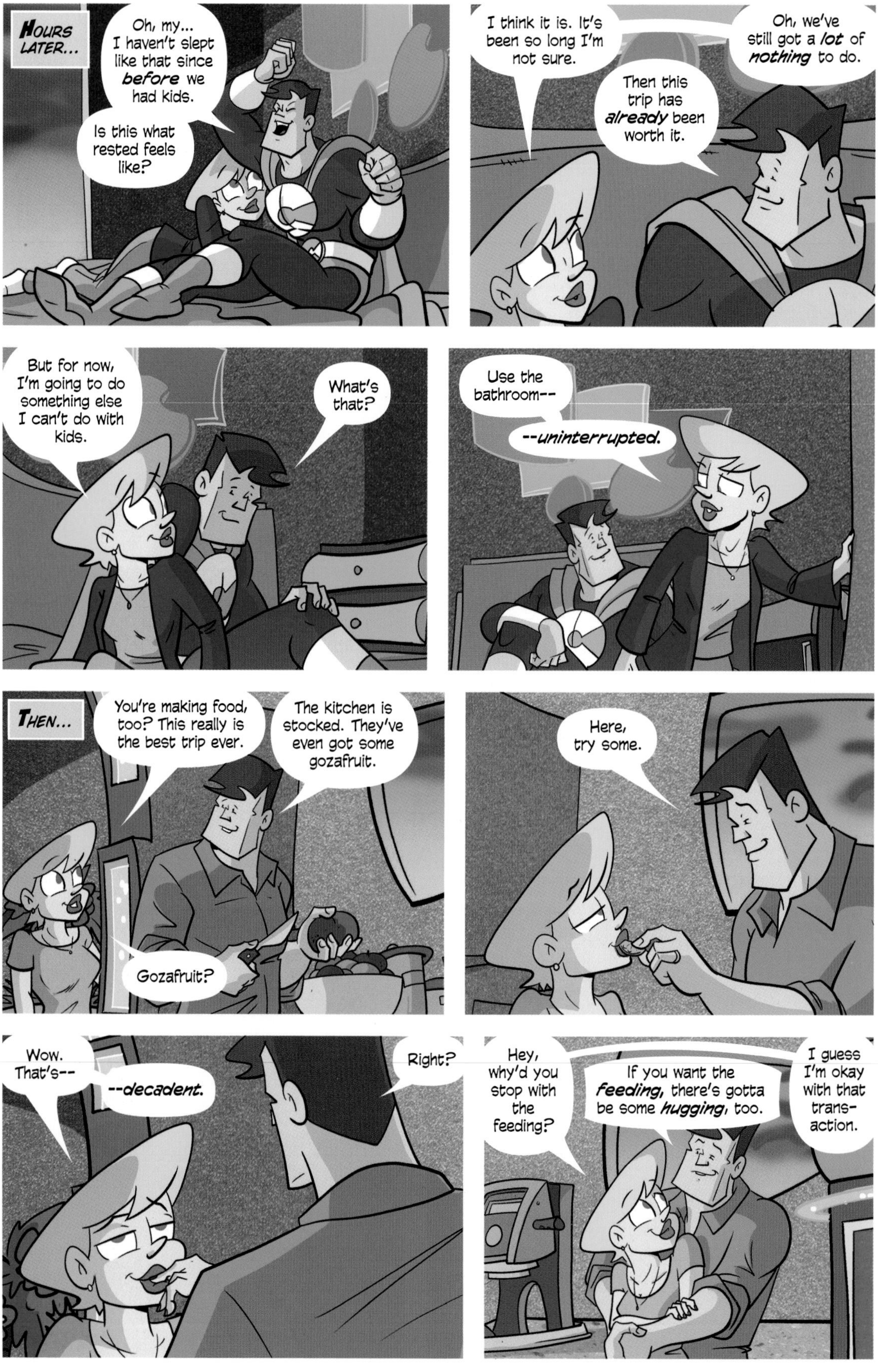

HOURS LATER...
Oh, my... I haven't slept like that since *before* we had kids.
Is this what rested feels like?
I think it is. It's been so long I'm not sure.
Oh, we've still got a *lot* of *nothing* to do.
Then this trip has *already* been worth it.
But for now, I'm going to do something else I can't do with kids.
What's that?
Use the bathroom--
--*uninterrupted.*
THEN...
You're making food, too? This really is the best trip ever.
The kitchen is stocked. They've even got some gozafruit.
Gozafruit?
Here, try some.
Wow. That's--
--*decadent.*
Right?
Hey, why'd you stop with the feeding?
If you want the *feeding,* there's gotta be some *hugging,* too.
I guess I'm okay with that trans-action.

BACK ON EARTH...

¿WAAAAH!¿

Do you need me to take her?

No, it's fine.

Let her cry her *warrior's cry* and warn her enemies that they should fear her wrath.

I have to say, I didn't know you'd be *so good* with kids, Zoe.

I used to watch my oldest sister's children. I have *some* experience.

And these two are so sweet.

And even when they're not, they're *still* pretty stinkin' cute.

It's their *true super power.*

3 DAYS of PEACE & MUSIC

THEN...

"With that, Melhawk placed the princess in the tower."

"'Oh no,' she cried. 'Who will come and save me?'"

Huh. I didn't realize this story was so... problematic.

You're a princess--

Past tense.

--did *you* ever need to be saved?

A *true* princess can *save herself.* I did it all the time.

Okay, James, we're going to get a little *William Goldman* here.

You *are* your mother's child.

Now, the Princess started looking for a way out...

The guy who wrote *Princess Bride?*

THE LIBERTY LEAGUE SATTELITE...

**Darkblade, what are *you* doing here?**

**When a *mysterious obelisk* lands in front of the White House, it's all hands on deck.**

**Well, I'm *glad* to have you here.**

**It's clearly a message, but from *whom?***

**Whatever it is, I can't *vibrate* through it.**

**Why would you send a message someone *can't read?***

**Maybe it's a *test.* Maybe they're warning *other* beings who can. I don't know.**

**Watching you two logic is *already* making my brain hurt. Is there anything *else* I can do to help?**

**Speed read a book on *codebreaking?* And bring me some *coffee.***

**I'll take an energy drink.**

THEN...

**I *know* there's a pattern here, Dagger, but I just can't see it.**

**Yeah, it's almost like it's *random--***

**--wait, no. That's it! It's a *fractal pattern.***

**See it?**

**It's a three dimensional pattern hopping from *side to side?***

**You're *right!* And from there it's a conjugated matrix!**

**So what does it say?**

**I haven't translated it *all,* but it starts:**

**"Prepare for *Lord Blackseed,* Prepare for *crisis.*"**

THEN...

Paul, are you *leaving?*

Yeah. Doc. I'm heading back to Chronopolis.

Blackseed is a *cosmic level* threat. I'm *street level.* .

You don't need me here.

Paul, your intellect and tactical prowess is *unmatched.*

You're right. Doc--

--it's been *exceeded.*

MEAN-WHILE...

Oh no!

What?

I just realized... I didn't *pack* for a royal gala! What am I going to *wear?*

More than the *kitchen* is stocked. There's a whole *closet* full of clothes for guests. I'm sure you can find something in there.

Okay. I'll take a look.

This isn't a closet. This is *warehouse.*

A *very interesting* warehouse.

Hmmmm.

THEN...

Abby? Did you manage to *find* something?

I *did*. Come take a look.

What do you think?

*That.*

You should wear that. *All* the time.

Leandian fashion is a *wonderful* thing.

Glad you think so--

--because I picked out an outfit for *you*, too.

THAT EVENING...

When's the last time we actually went to a party that didn't have *balloons* and a *caricature artist?*

Wait, no caricature artist? I'm *out* of here.

There *is* a bar though.

Well, then, maybe I'll stay.

Zashi! I'm glad you two made it.

So are we. Is the Queen around? We wanted to extend out appreciation.

Not *yet*, but she did express a desire to see you both. But she's still in negotiations.

*Still?* This must be serious.

She has to break a *deadlock*.

*Literally.*

THEN...

Mommy *never* lets me have chips on the couch.

Well, Aunt Charlotte is *much cooler* than your mom.

Just remember this when I'm *old* and need someone to *take care* of me.

Mrs. O? I--

--yes, I'm on it.

Charlotte, I *have* to leave. It's Paul. I'm sorry-

Don't be. *Go.*

But, uh, go through the *front door*.

I see why Mark misses that skylight so much.

THE LACROIX MANSION...

Mrs. O'Lonergan, I came as soon as I could.

I'm glad you came *at all.*

I didn't know *who else* to call.

You did the right thing. I think we *both* expected this.

We did.

What's happening here?

He doesn't let me *clean* anymore. He just spends all his time in the lair.

So he's there now?

He is.

≥Gasp!≤

Mrs. O, would you give us some space?

Zoe, I don't... what am I *even* doing?

Paul, are you all right?

I just... I *can't.*

All I had left was my *brain.* And that's not even enough. I'm just...I don't even know. *Why* am I here? What am I doing?

He *beat me,* Zoe. Dagger saw something I missed completely. He should just take my cape--

Paul.

That's *not* what this is about.

You *trained* Dagger. He's supposed to succeed you. That's the natural order. You should be proud. You *are* proud.

Then *why* do I feel like this?

You tell me. Dagger's like a son replacing his father. Why does that *bother* you so?

My son...?

Come on, Paul, you can figure this out.

Because...

...because...

BECAUSE HE WAS SUPPOSED TO BE HERE!!

He was my *Dad* and he was *supposed* to be here! And he's *not.*

He *died,* Zoe. His heart gave out and it took *mine* with it.

He was supposed to be here for *me.* For you. For *the kids* we were going to have.

It's *not fair.*

No. It's not.

But life doesn't go the way you plan it. Not even for *you* and your *analytical brain.* Your father *should* be here.

And my mother *should* be able to hold her grandchild.

But even if the Council ever *does* readmit me, if I ever do get home, and if I ever do have a child--

--Mother *still* won't have the strength.

That's just the way it is.

I wrecked *everything,* Zoe. Us. My company. Everything.

I just kept hurting and *hurting* and lashing out. I ruined everything and I don't know what to do anymore.

Paul, we're super heroes--

--we *fix things.*

BACK IN LEANDIA...

I'm having a *great time,* Abby.

So am I. We should have done this a *long time* ago.

You know, I *love* our family. But I love spending time with you *alone,* too.

Me, too. It's been *too long* since we've danced. You're *so good* at it.

Well, I am very *light* on my feet.

*LATER...*

Well said, Lady Abigail.

Tell your wife we said "Zashi."

Nice talking to you, too.

This has been fun, but maybe it's time for us to *head back.*

Maybe. I just don't know that I'm ready for the night to *end.*

I *didn't* say it was going to end--

--I just said that I wanted to *leave.*

It's too bad we never saw the *Queen,* though.

I see *my* queen. That's all I need.

MUCH LATER...

CHING CHING!

Mark?! Is that the *door?*

Stay where you are. I'll *get rid* of *whoever* it is.

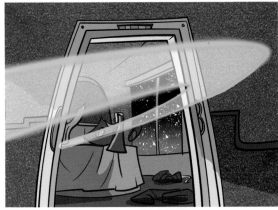

*Queen Oriana?*

Zashi, Sir Mark, I--

--I'm sorry, Mark, I'm interrupting.

No, no it's *fine.* You're not interrupting at all.

Please Mark, I'm a Queen, *not* an *idiot.*

And your shirt is on inside-out.

SHORTLY...

Lady Abigail, I am so sorry to interrupt.

Well, we *were* sorry not to see you.

The reason I wanted to see you both is that I have a mission that I *desperately* want you to accept.

I need you to act as my emissaries on a mission I can entrust to *no one else.* Will you accept?

Of course, your highness.

What do you need?

All I need is for you to make a *delivery* for me--

--in the *morning.*

Mrs. O, would you mind maybe getting us some tea?

Tea?

Oh, of course, child.

We'll be on the deck.

Thank you.

Wow. I forget sometimes.

Forget what?

The stars.

I've been staring into the dark for *so long* that I've been *missing* the *stars.*

Hey, is that--

--it *is!*

It's *Mark and Abby!*

Hey, I know I'm supposed to be helping Charlotte--

Zoe, don't worry. Everything's *fine.*

I *do* feel like we're interrupting something, though.

No. It's all good.

Yeah, that's what we said, too.

Your sister the Queen wanted us to bring *this* to you.

Wait--

--this is a *royal courier container*.

It *is*. And we're instructed to say:

On behalf of the royal court, we are informing you of *Edict 516*--

--which *changes* the royal charter so those who abdicate are *no longer* permanently banished from the kingdom of Leandia.

You're *no longer* in the line of succession and, as such, your former title can't be restored, of course.

So the Queen is granting you a *new one*...

...as of today, you are granted title and mission as *Leandia's Royal Ambassador to Earth*--

--LADY AMAZONIA.

:Sniff!: This is... this is *everything*.

I'm *so happy* for you.

I can go *home.*

You can go home.

And you finally found the perfect tiara.

Mark, Abby, *thank you* for bringing this.

It's our *absolute pleasure.*

But if you'll excuse us, we still have one more mission tonight.

We have to *rescue* Charlotte--

--from our *children.*

DECO CITY...

Hello, Charlotte!

Ypu're *back!* Did you have a good time?

We did!

It's *so quiet.* Is everything okay?

Yeah. Kids are in bed. I *wanded* Hayley and gave James a *bath*, too. They've been asleep for hours.

Charlotte, you're *amazing.*

After a weekend with the kids, we thought things would be a little more *frazzled.*

Please, I love my niece and nephew. They're a *joy.*

Beside, you forget--

--I'm *Charlotte-freakin'-Tennyson.*

124

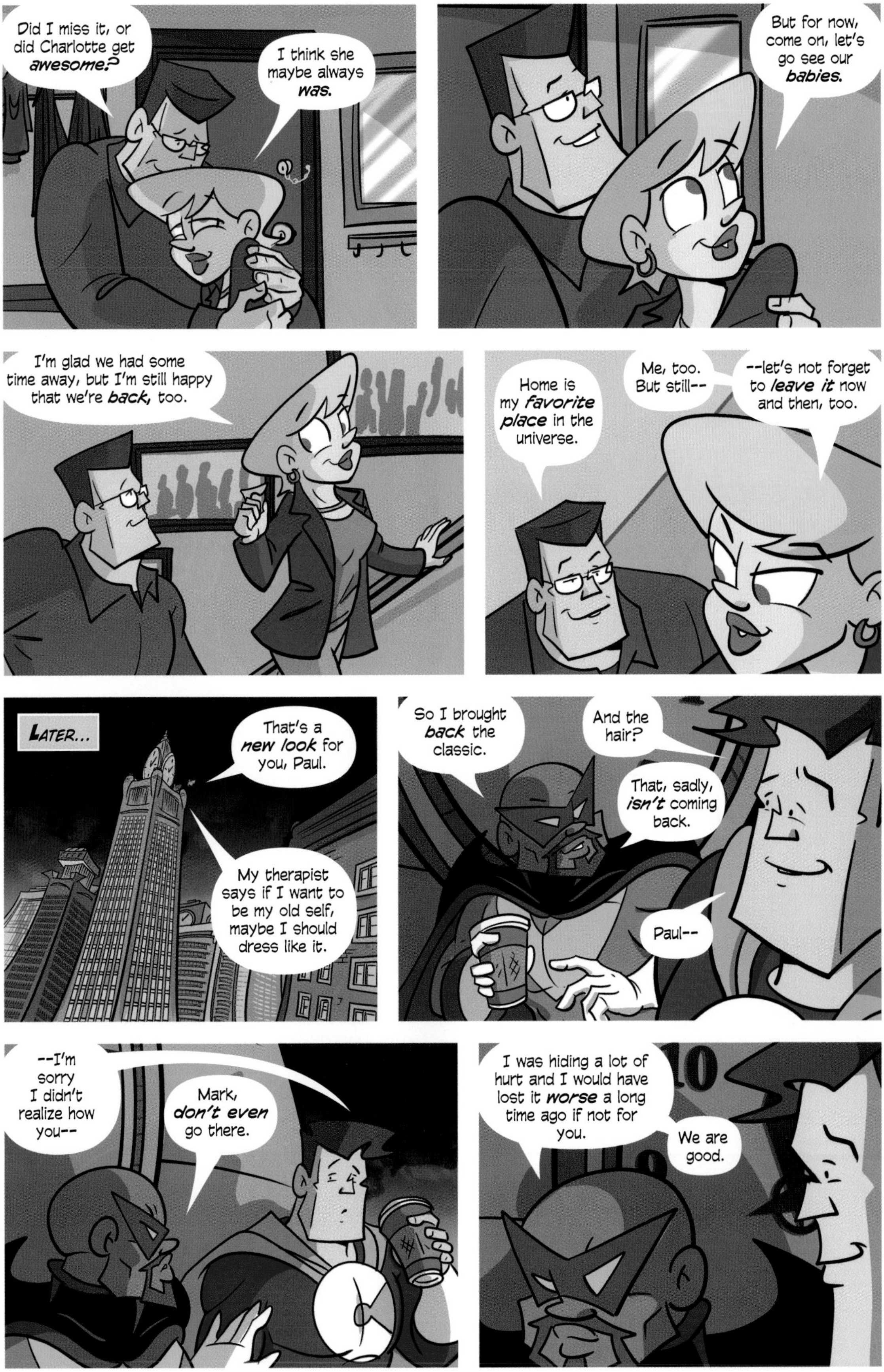
Did I miss it, or did Charlotte get *awesome?*
I think she maybe always *was.*
But for now, come on, let's go see our *babies.*
I'm glad we had some time away, but I'm still happy that we're *back,* too.
Home is my *favorite place* in the universe.
Me, too. But still--
--let's not forget to *leave it* now and then, too.
LATER...
That's a *new look* for you, Paul.
My therapist says if I want to be my old self, maybe I should dress like it.
So I brought *back* the classic.
And the hair?
That, sadly, *isn't* coming back.
Paul--
--I'm sorry I didn't realize how you--
Mark, *don't even* go there.
I was hiding a lot of hurt and I would have lost it *worse* a long time ago if not for you.
We are good.

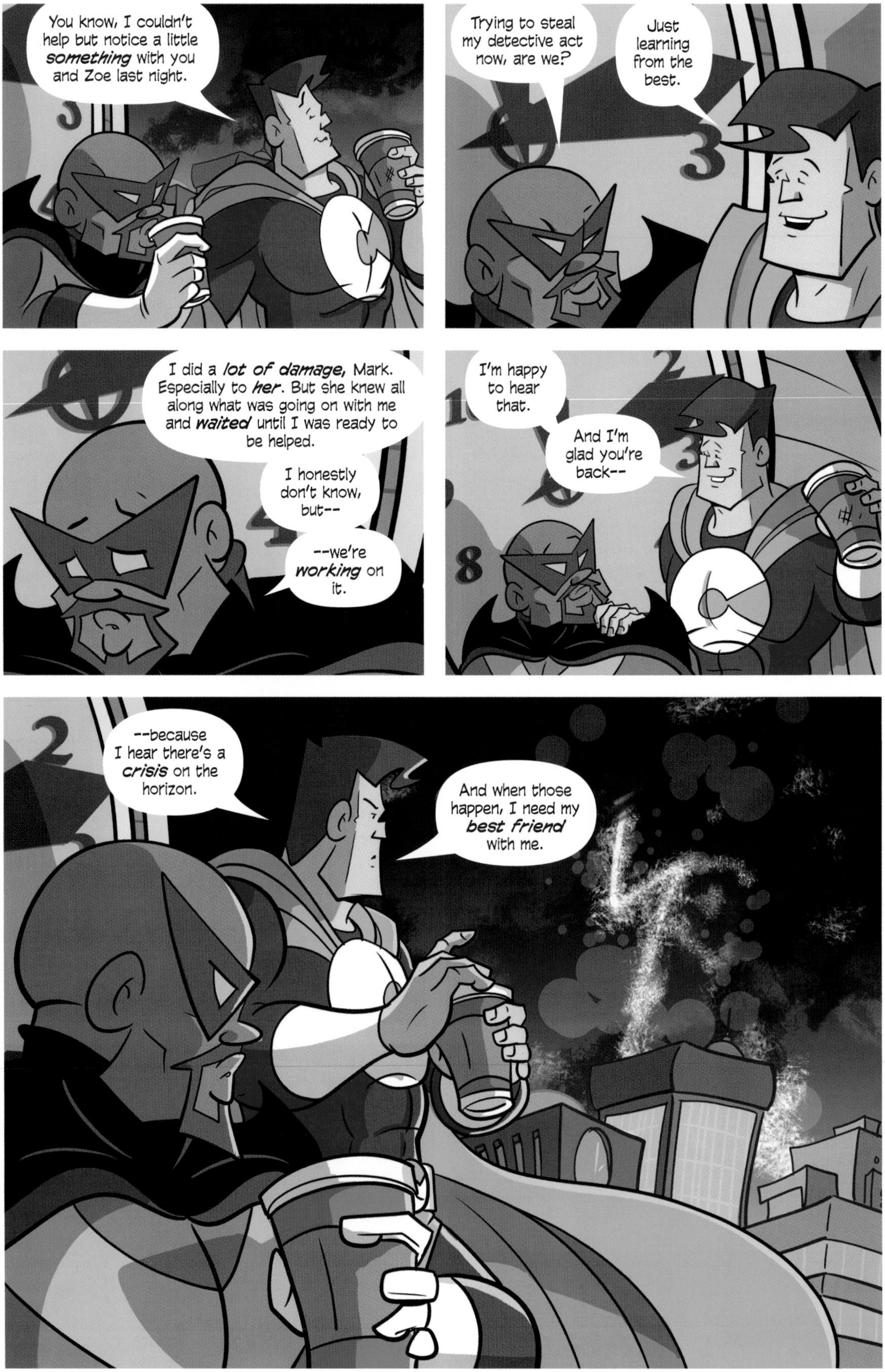
You know, I couldn't help but notice a little *something* with you and Zoe last night.
Trying to steal my detective act now, are we?
Just learning from the best.
I did a *lot of damage,* Mark. Especially to *her*. But she knew all along what was going on with me and *waited* until I was ready to be helped.
I honestly don't know, but--
--we're *working* on it.
I'm happy to hear that.
And I'm glad you're back--
--because I hear there's a *crisis* on the horizon.
And when those happen, I need my *best friend* with me.

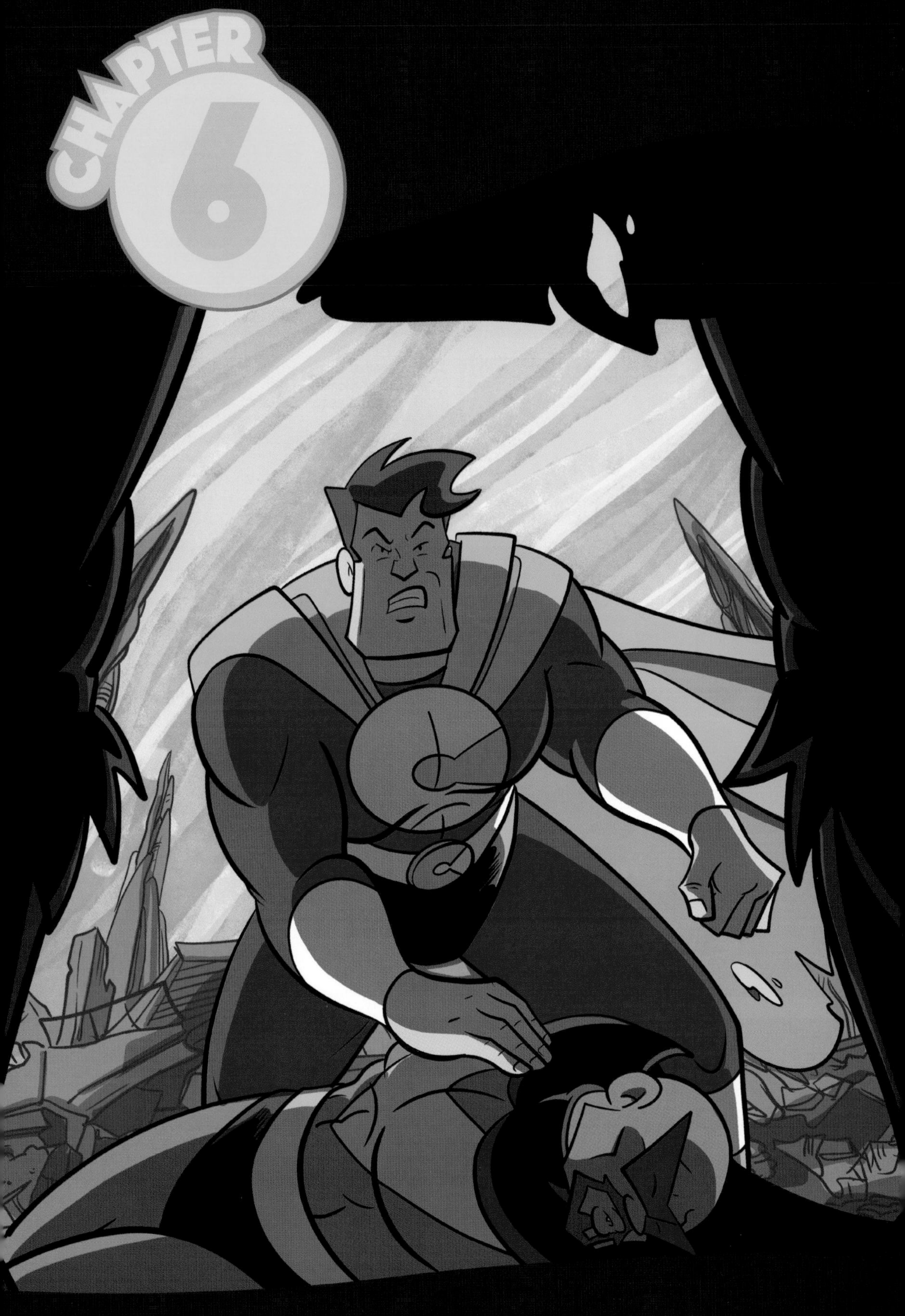
CHAPTER
6

"OH, AND I ENDED WORLD WAR TWO."

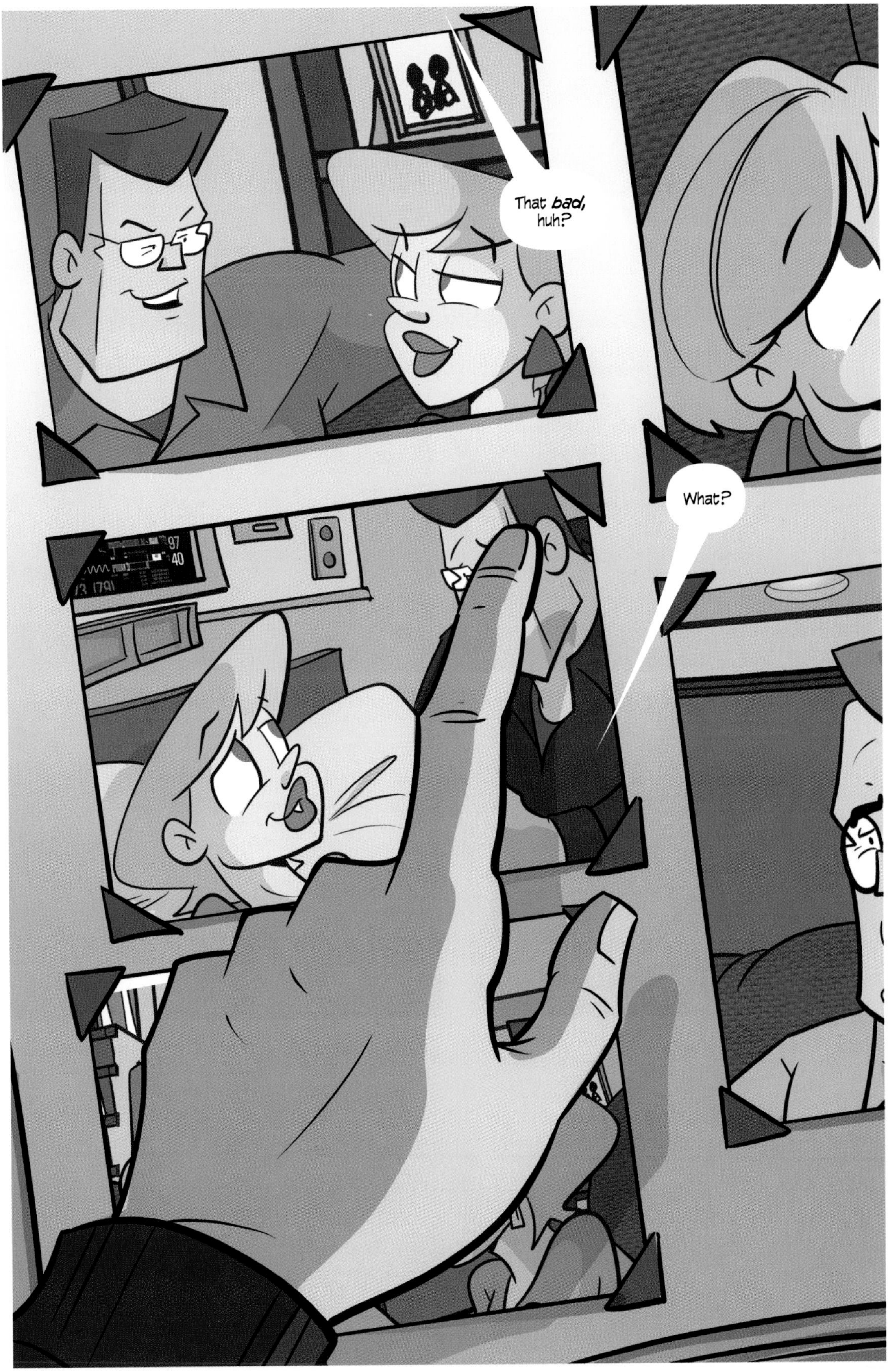

That *bad*, huh?
What?

You always go through the photo albums when something *bad* is coming.

I won't say it's bad but--it's *serious.* Blackseed is *pretty powerful.*

*You* might be worried but *I'm not.* I have great faith in my husband.

And it's fun to look at these photos. Even if they're a little *out of focus.*

You know it's *not* the photos with the focus problem, right?

Do you want my *glasses?*

So you're saying you're more scared of Blackseed than *me?*

**18** MONTHS AGO...

James has started singing his ABC's *all the time.* I think he'll be *reading* soon..

Between you and Abby, I don't doubt it.

I think *something's* wearing on Abby, though.

How so?

She's been a little *short* with me and James lately. It's *not* like her.

And she's *overslept* the last couple of days.

Well, she is *pregnant.*

*Later...*

He's *asleep*, right?

Put him to bed an hour ago.

You know, you're going to have to *stop* using that soon.

So let me *enjoy* it while I can.

How was Paul?

He was his *normal broody* self.

He did say something *funny*, though. We were talking and he said--

--he said you were *pregnant*.

I HAD A WHOLE THING PLANNED!

*Then...*

--and then I was going to come out with the *baby shoes*.

Oh, Abby, I'm sorry. I thought he was just *messing* with me.

It's just *ruined*.

Abby, it's *not* ruined. You're forgetting something *important*.

We're going to have another baby.

Yeah, we are.

A baby who will *not* be named Paul or Paulina.

Nope, that ship has sailed.

**THEN...**

Everything good?

Yes, Abigail.

All is well with the newest member of your family.

I will, of course, cast the same *power protection spell* as before. And this time I have the ingredients on hand.

The obvious question is, would you like me to discern the *sex* of your child this time?

We talked about it and...

...yes, as long as you can discern it *better* than that Enochian prophecy last year.

Enochian has a lot of *homophones*, all right?

Regardless-- Mark, Abigail, I am pleased to tell you...

...that in nine months...

...you will be welcoming a *daughter*.

A *girl!*

We're going to have a *girl!*

Can you imagine what *your* daughter will be like?

She'll probably be a superhero, a business owner, and the first *female president* of the United States.

Well, I'm kind of hoping she'll be the *second or third* by then.

THEN...

A *girl!* I have to admit, I was kind of hoping.

Me, too.

Mark, it'll be great...but it'll be *different,* too.

You were an *only child.* I had a brother *and* a sister.

Boys are louder and messier, but they're a little *easier* in some ways. You look at a girl the *wrong way,* and she'll burst into tears.

And we'll have *hair* and *dresses.* And *first dates.*

When *she* starts dating--

--that's when *I* reveal my identity to the world.

LATER...

So James, we have some *exciting news* for you.

Mommy's going to have *another baby.*

In a few months, *you're* going to have a *new baby sister.*

And *you* get to be a big brother! Isn't that exciting? Our family is going to get *bigger.*

Yeah! When do we pick her up from the *store?*

James, we don't get her from the store.

Oh, does *Am'zon* deliver her?

I bet a baby sister comes Prime.

He is *so* your son.

Yay, *free shipping.*

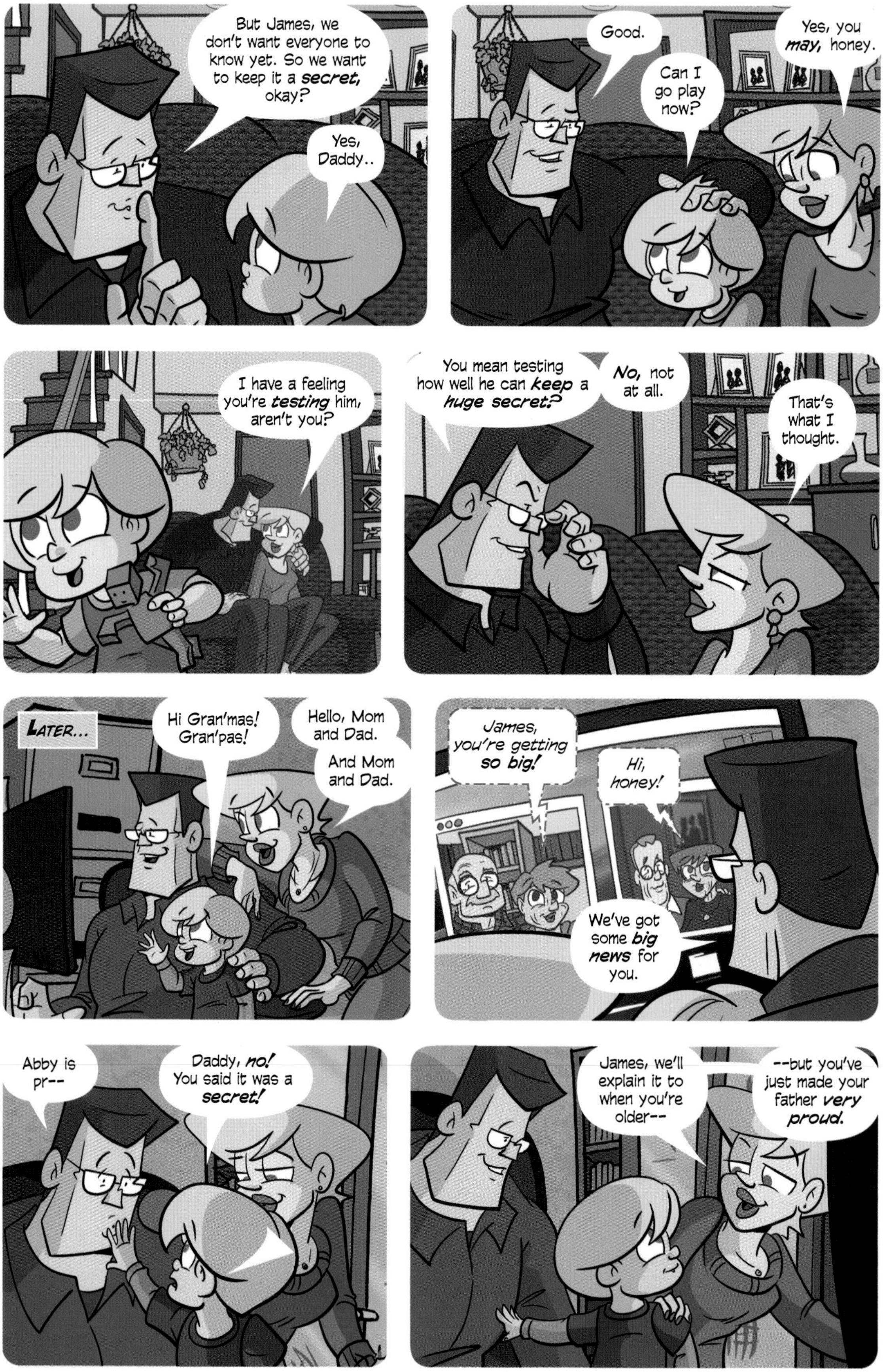

But James, we don't want everyone to know yet. So we want to keep it a *secret,* okay?
Yes, Daddy..
Good.
Can I go play now?
Yes, you *may,* honey.
I have a feeling you're *testing* him, aren't you?
You mean testing how well he can *keep* a *huge secret?*
*No,* not at all.
That's what I thought.
LATER...
Hi Gran'mas! Gran'pas!
Hello, Mom and Dad.
And Mom and Dad.
James, you're getting *so big!*
Hi, honey!
We've got some *big news* for you.
Abby is pr--
Daddy, *no!* You said it was a *secret!*
James, we'll explain it to when you're older--
--but you've just made your father *very proud.*

THEN...

He fell *asleep* again. I'm going to have to show him *Hercules* some other time.

He did skip his nap today.

You know...we're not going to have a *lot more* of these nights, are we?. Our family will be *bigger*. The odds will be *even*.

Well, kind of.

Mark, you've got *powers*. James *will* have them. Our daughter *will* have them. *I'm* the only one *without* powers.

That's not exactly even.

Abby, you're the mom--

--you've got *all* the power.

ONE YEAR AGO...

I think I'm going to need you to get my *maternity clothes* down. I'm definitely in Barnum and Bailey tent territory again.

Hey, what about *Bailey*? That's a *good name*. And a good *drink!*

Even leaving aside the idea of naming our daughter after a *liquor*, I'm not sure I want her to have the initials *B.S.*--

--but I like the *sound* of it. So what about *Hayley*?

Like the *comet*?

No, the Comet's name is *Steve*.

I don't want to call her Steve. *Hayley it is.*

*THEN...*

Charlotte! I thought *Abby* was going to bring me those auction items.

She was, but she decided *five flights of stairs* were a little beyond her today.

That's fair. How *is* everyone doing?

Everyone's *good.* Abby's tired, James is excited and Mark--

--well, he was getting on my nerves with his *overprotective father jokes.*

You know the "Any boy who comes to date my daughter will first have to survive my *handshake,*" flavor.

*Gah!* Why do earth men persist in treating their daughters like they are *fragile possessions?*

Perhaps I should *stand guard* and *intimidate* James's female suitors!

I don't know what that would do for his girl friends--

--but James would certainly have a *lot* more *guy friends.*

Well, I know Mark's attitude comes from a good pl--

--wait. *Why* are you looking at me like that?

Yeah, it's just...your *headpiece* is... um...

It looks like Pokemon ears.

Four years! *Four freaking years!*

Sorry.

But *cheer, up,* Zoe.

I'm sure your *next one* will be *the* one.

ONE YEAR AGO...

Crusader, do you see the *disturbance* yet?

Not yet. But I see a trail. Whatever it is came in came in *hot*.

I'm sure. Whatever it is, the quantum flux readings are *off the chart*.

Okay, I see it now. Going in closer.

It's--

--me?

Wow. I really *was* ruggedly handsome.

THEN...

So you're this world's Doctor Kismet?

*Karma.*

You are *definitely* a Mark Spencer from a parallel dimension.

What brought you here?

I was exploring the *Quantum Strand* and I guess I got too close. The next thing I knew... *zap*... I was here. And falling fast.

I was pretty out of it until you arrived.

The Strand is *pure quantum energy.* You absorbed enough that it altered your quantum signature and propelled you to *our* reality.

Unfortunately, you've also absorbed *too much* energy for mine magicks to remove.

You are *bound* here until those energies *dissipate.*

Looks like you're *stuck* here for a while, grandpa.

Don't think I won't put myself over my own *knee*, son.

LATER...

--you can bunk on the *satellite* until your multiversal block goes away.

But for now, I figured we could go to *my place*.

Sounds good.

So you've *never* been to a parallel earth before?

I never knew it was a thing.

I'm sure Doc Kismet mentioned a multiverse, but I only ever understood *half* of what he ever said.

Same here.

Are there a *lot* of differences?

Seems like everyone I know was born *sixty years earlier* than on your earth.

Past that, there are *little* things.

Like, my world's Mermantis has *yellow* gloves.

Oh, and I ended World War Two.

THEN...

Hello, honey!

So, Mark what was this *big surprise* you had?

Wait, who is *that?*

Abby, this is Mark Spencer from *Dimension-44*.

It's a world where we were *all* born in the 1920's.

Abby?

Oh, I've *missed* you.

Nice to *meet* you.

I'm *sorry.* That was forward--

It's okay. I'll take hugs from *any* Mark. *Regular* or *silver fox* edition.

**THEN...**

So *then* what?

Once we penetrated his Germanic shield, the *Sovereign Society* and I wrapped things up.

That's *awesome!*

Ooh! What about *me?*

You ran all the *scrap metal* and *other drives* for Deco City.

I met you and Charlotte at a *USO event,* in fact.

You spilled a box of *dance tickets* on the ground and it was just so *adorable* I fell in love.

Awww.

I gotta know. What was Charlotte like?

Oh, she was *indispensable* to the war effort.

Oh, you boys are *so sweet!*

Come on, let's head to the canteen!

I need a dance with *each one* of you!

Momm! Daaad! Can I have some *water?*

Here I'll take care of this.

Coming, James!

Actually, I'm *glad* he's leaving for a minute. There's something I wanted to talk to you about.

Um, sure.

Just--take it from an old man who's been there. Get him to *retire* at some point. *Give up* his powers and live a *normal life.*

You sound like you're speaking from *experience.*

I *am.* I wish I had done it.

Abby, I just turned *one hundred and one.*

How old do you think *you* were?

139

You didn't--you didn't *accidentally* hit that dimensional barrier, did you?

You always knew me so well.

Abby, I'm *lonely* and I miss my wife. I guess the good thing is that I get to see her again in *you*.

I'm *glad* I can remind you of her. And I'm *definitely* going to tell my Mark when I can. That's good advice.

But you...

If your Abby were here, she *wouldn't* want you to be sad. She'd want you to find a new mission...do something with your *extraordinary life*.

You've given me and my Mark some *good advice*.

Maybe the multiverse can use an *elder statesman*.

MEANWHILE...

And here's Darkblade, buddy.

Thanks, Dad!

Hey, Dad. When I have a sister, will you still *tuck me in* and *read to me?*

James, when she's born, the baby will definitely need a lot of *attention*--

--but your mom and I will *always* be here for *you*, too.

You know what *else* your sister will need?

What?

Her *big brother*.

You know what else she might need, too?

What?

A *puppy*.

Keep trying, son.

TODAY...

Thank you all for coming. Most of you *already* know that *Lord Blackseed* is planning an attack on Earth.

This meeting will address *who* he is and *what* we're going to do about it.

We'll split into *two teams*. Street level heroes will keep the civilians safe and handle collateral damage.

*Cosmic powers* will fight him and his shock troops.

Blackseed is the megalomaniacal ruler of a planet in the Andromeda galaxy. He has attacked Earth before, but this is his *first time* personally leading the charge.

He is a *Zeta Level* power.

Well, I know of *another* Zeta Level power in training.

Well, get her or him *here*.

Unfortunately, right now we're mostly training her to sleep through the night.

Blackseed is a big threat, but we've beaten his kind before. With *all of you*, I'm *sure* we'll come through this fine.

Dismissed.

*Amazonia*, I'd like a moment before you leave.

Yes, Paul?

Zoe, look, I know we're still *figuring out* things between us... but if this goes *bad*, I wanted to--

--!

Now you've got something to *live* for.

Come back *alive* or you'll have to answer to me.

Under-stood.

LATER...

I'll see you two when I *get back* from my trip.

You be *good* for your mother, James.

I'll do what I can.

I will, Dad. Have a good conven'shun.

Good night, Dad!

Good night, James!

Come to Aunt Charlotte, sweetie.

You told him you were going to a *comic convention?*

Seemed accurate.

I mean, I'll be with lots of people in *costume* fighting for *space.*

Good night, Hayley. I'll see you soon.

Charlotte, *thanks* for your help. But can I ask you *another* favor?

Sure!

What do you need?

I wanted to show you something in my costume closet.

This is a *dimensional portal.* If you get a signal from me, activate it and get Abby and the kids to Leandia.

Mark, she's *not* going to want to go without you.

Charlotte, if you get that signal--

--I'm *already gone.*

Mark, I *know* this is serious. And you're the *main line* of defense, right?

So I have an *idea*.

Yes.

You could have Doctor Karma give *me* powers, like he did for Abby* and then I could help you out.

There'd be *two* of us, and then we could swoop in and *smash* Blackseed.

* Love and Capes Vol. 1, #10.

Charlotte it *doesn't* quite work like that.

And then I could start policing people who drive *slow* in the *fast lane*.

Charlotte...

And then I'd find *cheating* Adam Douglas and wrap his *stupid convertible* around a *tree*.

What's going on here?

I'm learning that with great imagination comes great irresponsibility.

THEN...

I'll let myself out. Give me a shout if you need me.

Thanks, Charlotte.

Mark, how worried should I be?

*Nothing* I say is going to make you stop worrying, so I'm *not* going to try. But look, I'm with the *best group* of people to handle exactly this kind of thing.

And heck, even Charlotte gave me an *idea* that might help, too.

*Charlotte* gave you an idea?

It really *is* the end of the world, isn't it?

10 MONTHS AGO...

Abby what--?

Now? Are you sure?

Your water broke?

That's actually kind of ironic, but I don't think you'd appreciate it right now.

Get Charlotte to take you and I'll be there as soon as--

--wait, what do you mean you fixed it?

Hey, there.

Need a hand?

MEAN-WHILE...

Jason, Abby just went into labor. I have to take her to the hospital.

Can you hold down the fort?

Sure! But where's Mark?

Wait, she said. Let me check...

WHEEL OF EXCUSES
a LaCroixTech app

SPIN

Um...

Oh! His car broke down across town.

Man, that guy has the worst luck sometimes. She's lucky she has you.

She really is. Not all heroes wear capes, you know.

144

SHORTLY...

Okay, we're all set, Abby.

Abby! Am I *in* time?

Always. Everything's good and I'm all settled in. And I'm glad you're *here*.

How are you doing?

I'm fine and I'm ready for everything. *Except* for the pain.

They say the body *forgets* pain.

It would explain why women go through this *more* than once.

Well, it's *all* coming back to me now.

**18** HOURS LATER...

It's time, Abby.

≳Huff!≲ Finally.

James's labor was a *lot* shorter.

You *said* girls were harder.

Besides, this is perfect *guilt material* for your mother-daughter arguments.

Now push.

*Push!*

Here we go. Welcome to the multiverse--

--Hayley Catherine.

She's *perfect!*

Yes, she is.

Nice work, Doctor.

Always a pleasure, Doctor.

*LATER...*

Mark, I'm just gonna close my eyes...

You *go ahead.* I'm going to step outside for a minute.

Thanks for the assist yesterday, sir.

My pleasure, son. But you'll have to catch the *next one* yourself.

You're *leaving?*

That quantum energy has finally dissapated. I can go *home.*

You don't *have to,* you know.

No, I do. Too many ghosts here. Besides, I've got a *new mission* thanks to your Abby.

She's a *special one.*

She is indeed. In any universe.

Keep 'em flyin'!

TODAY...

Mommy!

It's okay James. It's probably just thunder.

Now it's still *your turn*. Go ahead and roll.

You'd better roll *big*, squirt! I'm going to catch up with you.

Are *you* okay, Char?

How do you *do it*, Abby? I saw Mark. He was *shaken*. He's worried. Why aren't *you*?

Because he's my husband. It's my job to believe in him enough for the *both* of us--

"--so he can be the man he *needs* to be."

STAND DOWN, CRUSADER!

STAND DOWN AND *I* WILL GRANT YOU A MERCIFUL END.

IT IS TIME TO DRAW THE CURTAIN ON THIS PERFORMANCE SO THIS WORLD'S NEXT ACT CAN BEGIN.

See, that's where you're wrong, Blackseed.

You think I'm the *finale*--

--but I'm just the *opening act.*

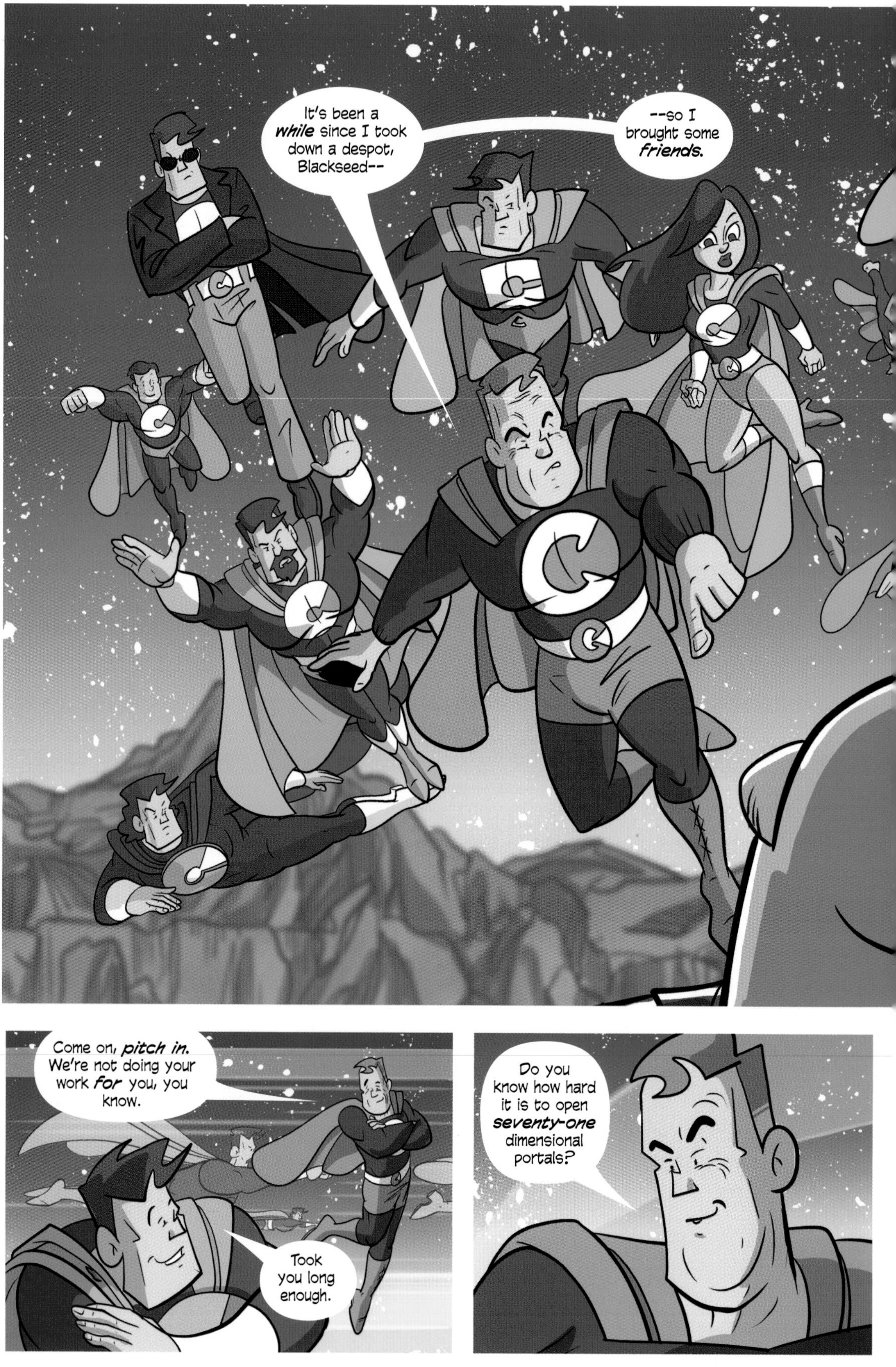
It's been a *while* since I took down a despot, Blackseed--
--so I brought some *friends.*
Come on, *pitch in.* We're not doing your work *for* you, you know.
Took you long enough.
Do you know how hard it is to open *seventy-one* dimensional portals?

I can't say as I do.

Me *neither*, but the Doctors Karma and Kismet certainly complained about it.

Did I see a version of us that's a *cat?*

Believe it or not, his name is *Marrrk Spencpurr.*

THEN...

Many hands really *do* make light work, don't they?

They do. Thanks for coming.

Our pleasure. Besides, *your* universe is where this all started.

Your Abby got me to thinking that maybe I could share some insights with *other* Crusaders *throughout* the Multiverse.

That's why there's even a *Congress of Crusaders* at all.

You look *beat*, son. And it's no surprise. You held the line until we could get here.

Get yourself *home* to your wife. *We'll* take care of the rest of this.

An honor fighting alongside you, Crusader.

The honor is all mine, sir.

ELSEWHERE...

It looks like the *last Crusader* has left our dimension.

Sure, they get the easy job. We get *shock troop clean up.*

Still, it's great that he has a *Myriad of Marks* to consult with.

Right? I wish *I* had a Board of Darkblades. Maybe they could have set me *straight* and I *wouldn't* have sold off my company.

You *were* decidedly off your game, weren't you?

You never bothered to see *who* was buying your company, did you?

Wait-- you...?

The Lady Amazonia, *majority shareholder* of LaCroix Consolidated. Pleased to meet you.

You bought *everything?*

Well, MausHaus outbid me for your film library.

But I still have everything else. Including the *studio* itself.

You know, I have been looking for someone to *run* that for me. Would you be *interested?*

We could talk about it... *over dinner.*

Dinner?

Yeah... that would be *great.*

Hey, does that mean you bought Catch 201 as well?

You think I'd let our *favorite restaurant* fall into anyone else's hands?

Though, if you had taken much longer to come to *your senses* I would have turned it into a Chipotle.

**ELSEWHERE...**

Mark!

I see you opened the wine. Our victory made the news, then?

It did.

How are you, sweetie?

Tired. So very *very* tired.

Well, that explains you using the skylight.

Sorry. I just was too beat to--

It's all right. Everything's fine.

CHIP-CHIRP!

Well, *almost* everything.

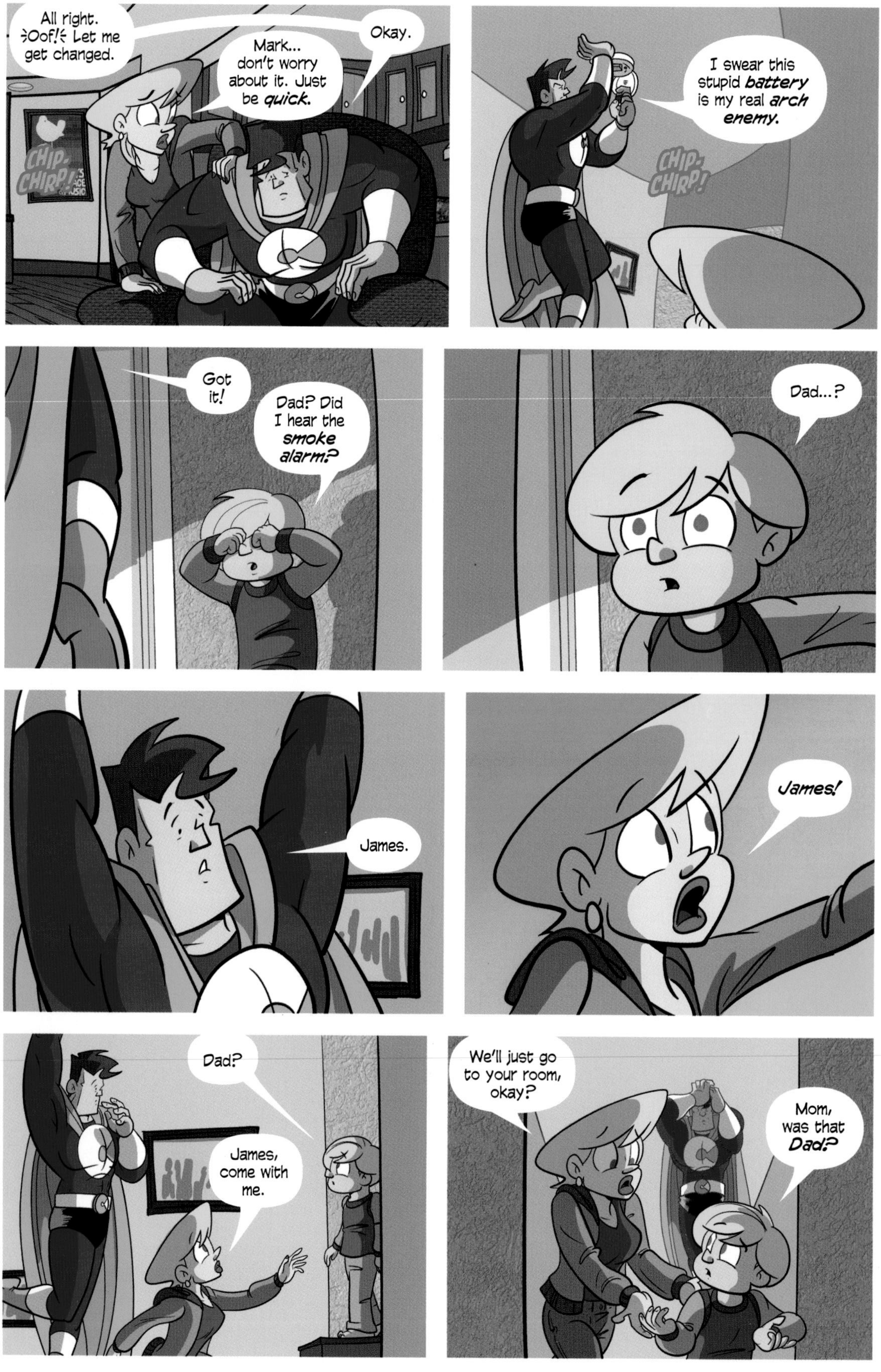
All right. Oof! Let me get changed.
Mark... don't worry about it. Just be *quick*.
Okay.
CHIP-CHIRP!
I swear this stupid *battery* is my real *arch enemy*.
CHIP-CHIRP!
Got it!
Dad? Did I hear the *smoke alarm?*
Dad...?
James.
*James!*
Dad?
James, come with me.
We'll just go to your room, okay?
Mom, was that *Dad?*

He's in his room for now.

What did you tell him?

I just told him to *wait* for us.

I'm *so sorry.* I should have *heard* him... I should have been faster... I was just so tired.

Mark, it's okay. I *told* you to do it.

And we knew this was going to happen *eventually.*

Still, I would have rather he just *walked in* on us.

*That would not have been better!*

He's waiting. *What* are we going to do?

Doc Karma could *erase* his memory, right?

Or maybe we convince him it was a *dream?*

Abby...

...look, eventually we *are* going to tell him. And he's going to know we outright *lied* to him in this moment.

Not just the *cutesy lies* like where I disappear to, but *really lied.*

I don't want to *lie* to our son *like that.*

Neither do I.

Why don't I bring him to the roof? And you should change into a *new uniform.*

You're right, he should see me at my *best.*

And also *not* smelling like *peat moss.*

AND SO...

James--

--this is your father.

Dad?

Yep. I'm your Dad.

And I'm also *the Crusader.*

We're *sorry* you found out this way. We were always going to tell you. But you're still *so young.*

I guess we need you to *grow up* a little faster tonight.

My Dad's the Crusader.

Awesome.

James, your father keeps his identity secret to protect not just *him* but all of *us*, too.

Me. You. Hayley. *Everyone.*

And it's *really important* that we *keep* that secret, okay?

You're now part of the special club that *protects the Crusader.* Can you do that?

I can do that.

We know you can.

And this club *isn't* just the three of us. You should know who *else* is in it.

*Both* sets of your grand-parents know. And *Aunt Charlotte.*

What about Uncle Quincy?

Unfortunately.

*Mark--!*

This is *way* past your bedtime, though. We should probably get downstairs--

*Wait!*

James, I know you have a *lot* of questions. And we'll answer each and every one of them.

But first there's something I want to do.

Something I've wanted to do since the *day* you were *born.*

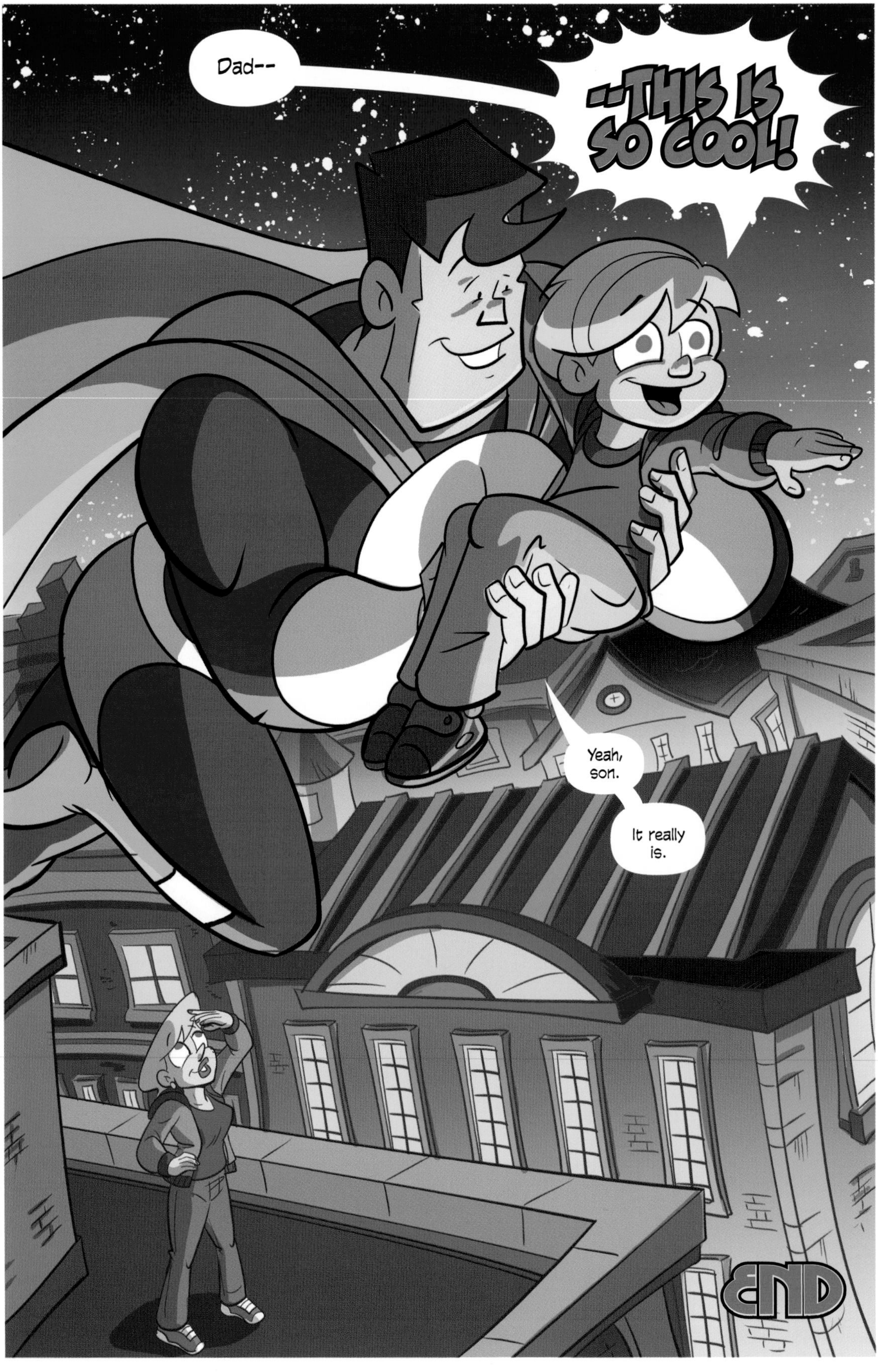
Dad--
--THIS IS SO COOL!
Yeah, son.
It really is.
END

# BEHIND THE SCENES

**I WAS JUST HAVING A HAMBURGER.**

It was Grand Rapids Comic-Con in 2018. And I'm at dinner with a bunch of friends after the show. Among these friends was Greg Weisman, creator of the *Young Justice* cartoon. And Greg says, kind of sheepishly, kind of conspiratorially: "Can I ask you a question?"

"Sure," I said, a little nervous. I thought he was going to ask something deep or dark. Like what happened to me during those five years on that island in the Pacific.

"Are you ever coming back to *Love and Capes?*"

Well, that wasn't the question I was expecting.

So I told Greg what I told anyone who asked me that, and there have been a few before him, that I would come back to *Love and Capes* when I had a story to come back for. I wasn't "done" with it, I wasn't over it, I just got to where I wanted to, was really happy with the landing, and didn't want to overstay my welcome.

But, unlike anyone else, Greg had a follow-up. "I have an idea," he said.

And then I replied what anyone else would. "Okay, Greg Weisman, who's written *Young Justice* and *Captain Atom* and the good season of *Rebels*... what's your idea?" Chuckle. Snort.

*THE ORIGINAL PROMOTIONAL GRAPHIC, POSTED TO INSTAGRAM ON VALENTINE'S DAY 2019.*

"I'd jump it a few years and now Mark and Abby have two kids."

I thought about it for a hot second and realized *that solves all my problems.*

You see, any time I thought about coming back to *Love and Capes* and continuing the story, I kept running into a brick wall. I didn't know how to end it. I didn't know how to walk away.

I think stories should have endings. And, without getting too dark, I know that I only have a finite amount of time to tell stories. I don't want to leave something horribly unfinished, like *Dune* or *Wheel of Time* or like, inevitably, *Game of Thrones*. So, when I sign on to a story, I want to sign on to having an ending.

The idea of coming back to Mark and Abby's family left me without a good stopping point. The original series was dating to engaged to married and ending with their first child. So where did I aim for? First birthday? Starting school? Graduating college? That's twenty-two years of stories. I don't know if I have that in me.

And adding to the level of difficulty, the story wouldn't be about Mark and Abby anymore. It'd be Mark and Abby **and** James. It's no longer *Mad About You*... it's *Mad About Us.*

But...

But if I jumped ahead, then I could also hopscotch around the kids' lives, too. I could do newborn jokes with the new kid and older stuff with James. And I could break up Darkblade and Amazonia, too. Hey, this could work. I just needed an ending. It'd have to be something big, something worth coming back for…

Well, kids, that's getting ahead in the story. But first let me tell you about how I met your Aunt Robin.

# IT ALWAYS STARTS WITH COFFEE

### IT SEEMS LIKE A LOT OF MY WORK HAPPENS AT CONVENTIONS.

Probably because I do so many. But, at a lull at my table, I started figuring out how to bring them back. There had to be a structure to it. I'd start with the coffee joke so that we could build up to the first appearance of the Crusader in five years. I wanted you to hear the music swell. And explain how you can pick up coffee at super-speed.

COMING UP WITH BAD HEADPIECES WAS ALMOST AS HARD AS COMING UP WITH A GOOD ONE.

Then a Crusader and Darkblade scene, so you know there's something wrong with Paul and that there might be trouble with his relationship. And then show what we **think** is baby James but turns out to be their second child. Which is a huge surprise if you skipped the cover, I suppose, but I still wanted the reveal. And then we've got the new setup.

You may notice that Darkblade and Amazonia's costumes look like their alternate universe versions from issue #12. Back then, the concept was that without Mark, Darkblade got darker and Zoe had to grow up.

With them broken up, Paul got darker, so his costume got darker. And Zoe, well with her, it was two things. The first is that yes, she's become more mature and her costume reflects that. The other is that the ridiculous '90s excessive costume that I gave Zoe just didn't feel as funny any more.

The one thing I couldn't figure out was a new headpiece for her. It's why she didn't wear one in the last issue and ultimately when I couldn't think of one, that's when I decided to make her constant quest for one to be the running gag. If I couldn't come up with a solution, then neither could she.

Besides, I knew what she'd be getting to replace it.

I made sure to reference everyone just so you knew who was okay. Mark's parents make an appearance. Abby's mom makes an appearance, and calls her husband. And Quincy gets name-checked, too.

My hardest challenge was my aversion to exposition. So, there's no great way to set up the Spencer kids' daycare arrangements. Basically, Abby works less at the store so she's home a couple days a week, Charlotte takes a day, their mother takes a day, and Mark takes a day. A day when I'm sure Abby is ready to run back upstairs.

And I introduced the idea that Hayley has powers, too, without giving her actual powers… yet. It's hard to discipline a kid with super powers. I don't have a solid plan for what exactly her powers will be, but I am now convinced she's the power source that sends James/Titan back from the future at the end of *What to Expect*.

And, by the end, we know that Paul and Zoe are broken up. Our new normal is set up.

I wanted to show some progression on all the characters since the last time. Some are minor, like Mark having different glasses. Abby has a shorter haircut. Paul is bald with a goatee. Zoe has no tiara. (Actually, both Amazonia and Darkblade look a little bit like their alternate-reality counterparts for *Love and Capes* #12, where he was broken up by Crusader's death and Amazonia had to become more mature to fill his shoes.) All their parents have grayer hair.

Also changed? The word balloons. Now they're solid white, not transparent.

Charlotte is the one who changes the least. Her hair is a little shorter, but probably not enough to be noticed. It's okay, though, because you don't need to fix awesome.

# YOU STILL HAVE TO GIVE OUT CANDY

CHARLOTTE'S GENDER-FLIPPED DEAN FROM *SUPERNATURAL* AND JASON AS, WELL, JASON ARE STILL FUNNY TO ME.

I READ AN ARTICLE THAT SAID THAT AFTER *STAR WARS: THE FORCE AWAKENS* A NUMBER OF BOYS BORN WERE NAMED "KYLO."

And I thought "Well, clearly their fathers weren't involved in that decision."

That became the genesis of the running gag about Mark not liking that James was going to dress like Kylo Ren.

It was important to me that in the finale, Mark doesn't dress like Crusader. It always bothered me when super heroes would dress like their secret identity for Halloween, especially when they used their real costume. Those super-hero costumes have to be so outrageously good compared with store-bought ones that it'd be suspicious. Think of what a costume looks like in a Marvel movie compared to what you buy at a Target. So when Mark dresses like Dagger, it had to be a cheesy one.

Though, as someone who grew up on Ben Cooper costumes, holy moley are store-bought costumes awesome these days.

The end, where Paul sees Mark's kids dressed as Darkblade and Amazonia is to show his lingering kid issues. That was a scary thing to do, because we had to feel the emotion without knowing why for a story that wouldn't be paid off for three more issues.

This issue laid a lot of groundwork. Darkblade is getting a little darker and more violent and not being completely honest. Amazonia is still trying to get back home, but we also establish that her friends have been able to go back on her behalf. And that smoke detector joke will pay off somewhere else, too.

Also, I hope this was the regulation and licensing comedy that everyone was waiting for.

# SLEEP? THAT'S WHERE I'M A VIKING!

I REMEMBER SITTING AT DINNER WITH MY FRIENDS, TALKING ABOUT THESE NEW *LOVE AND CAPES* ISSUES.

"I figured out what was going on with everyone," I said, "except Quincy." And as soon as I said it, I knew what he was up to. Of course he'd be using Mark to meet women. But we also see that he's been somewhat respectful of knowing Mark's secret. And that he can still play Mark.

In this issue, Mark is running around way too much, traveling too much, and keeping an insane schedule. Completely unrelated, I do a lot of conventions and traveling, and was writing and drawing two different comics, plus the occasional *My Little Pony* or *Star Trek* comic.

The whole sleep-deprived Mark event was set up way back in *Love and Capes: Ever After* #4 where Mark establishes that he needs to sleep and if something goes weird, Darkblade can stop him.

The cover parodies both Dark Knight and the Nick Cardy Aquaman/Black Manta cover. I worked hard to make the name Martha be as much like that cover as possible. And, obviously, the Martha Jefferson/Martha Washington joke is a riff on *Batman v Superman*. Hey, maybe Mrs. Jefferson and Washington were the same person…?

It was fun showing how much Mark works and his slow descent into madness. And my favorite sequence is him trapped on the couch with his family (where he's apparently watching the *Cupid's Arrows* TV show which also features a cameo by my *Warning Label* characters… references upon references).

Also, in the borrowing from my life section… I don't like soup.

# I LIKE LIVING UP HERE

SO, NOW IT CAN BE REVEALED WHO THE MISSING MEMBER OF MARK'S SECRET IDENTITY SOCIETY IS.

It's Father Jerry. Back in *Love and Capes: Ever After* #2, Mark and Abby tell her parents that X people know who he is. Charlotte, Mrs. O, Mark's parents… but there's someone unaccounted for.

Father Jerry is totally based on a parish priest from my childhood. He was (and is) awesome. His homilies were peppered with humor and He-Man references. He taught me a lot about my faith, but also storytelling and public speaking. To take a serious subject and still have fun with it has permeated my work for years. (And I've

I'M SURE MARK REVEALED HIS IDENTITY UNDER THE SEAL OF THE CONFESSIONAL.

remained in touch with him over the years, too.)

I enjoyed giving the Crusader a magical imp character as a pest, and it took forever to think of exactly the perfect trivia question. The scene also establishes that Paul has sold his movie studio to MausHaus, furthering his descent into self-destruction.

But more than anything, I also wanted this to be an Abby-heavy story, because it was time for her to be in the spotlight. I wanted to show her as a businesswoman and a mother and how things have changed for her. I think we all compare ourselves to our peers, so I created a peer for Abby who was more successful. Well, more successful in at least *some* aspects.

No one has the same mix of success. And you need to find the mix that works for you to be your success.

I also like showing how Abby has matured over the years, and that she was a little more wild in high school and college.

By the way, the "Harvey" that Bria is talking to? Harvey Spector from *Suits*. Because man do I love me that show.

And I love expanding the super-hero universe. Steel Worker was seen way back in *Love and Capes* #7, and it was great to flesh him out. Obviously he's inspired by Iron Man, but I love the idea that he's a garage mechanic working out of his house.

# THINGS GET REAL

### FIRST, I LOVE DRAWING LEANDIA.

I love designing a place that has the design aesthetic of the 1980 Flash Gordon film. Bright colors, ridiculous costumes, and more.

I also wanted to show that both Zoe and Charlotte are willing parts of the lives of Mark and Abby's kids. There were no "bad babysitter" jokes here. While they're all different, they're all good at it.

Mark's aversion to travel has been a running gag and came out of a truncated idea that they would visit MausPark and they'd have to drive. But the ending of the series upends that setup, so I wanted to use it here.

THE RUNNING STORYLINE OF MARK'S FATHER'S HIP REPLACEMENT AND REHAB HELPS SHOW HIS PARENTS GETTING OLDER.

This issue also did the big reveal of what happened to Darkblade. His father died, and he was so wounded that he pushed everyone else away, becoming Darkerblade. And among the things I love about this arc is Zoe's reaction throughout. She knows what's happening. She knows why it's happening. And she is the most mature she's ever been.

She's sad about it and she hasn't been waiting or pining for him. Even though she's, as she says, a "Dry Spell Debutant," she's clearly tried to date now and then. But she's always hoped that she and Paul would reunite.

Both she and Mrs. O expected that Paul would eventually have this breakdown sometime. And she was ready with it to bring him through it. Not Mark, but Zoe.

Which is a huge change for both characters.

And, as if to reward that act of growth, after five years, Zoe is finally allowed to return to Leandia.

This issue is one of the great examples of "It's easy to write a note that says 'Darkblade has a breakdown,' but much harder to execute." Eventually, I came up with the idea that all Paul has had to lean on was his super heroing and his, as Lin-Manuel Miranda would say, top-notch brain. Once he gets shown up, that's when everything falls apart. I think it worked well for him.

# SINCE THE DAY YOU WERE BORN

THIS ISSUE'S ENDING IS WHY I RETURNED TO *LOVE AND CAPES*.

Mark, exhausted from some adventure, comes home and is accidentally revealed to be the Crusader to his son. They figure out what to do, decide to tell him, and it ends with Mark taking his son for a flight. That ending felt big enough to come back for. That's why there's this new volume.

Thematically, that ending came from a discussion I heard on one of Merlin Mann's podcasts (*Due By Friday*, I think. But it could have been *Reconcilable Differences*). It was about how his daughter learned the truth about Santa Claus and how he handled it. What he did was make her part of the club. It was now her job to preserve the magic for other people, and she was part of a special group. It made her not want to spoil things for everyone else, and keep the secret in the best way. I thought that was beautiful, and perfect for Mark and Abby to use with James. He's not in trouble. He's not read the riot act. Instead, he's now part of a secret society.

Figuring out what would wreck Mark was a lot harder. After watching *Avengers: Endgame* and DC-TV's *Crisis on Infinite Earths,* I had to do my own crossover.

And the idea for Old Mark comes from my love of DC's Earth-Two. I liked the idea of an older, wiser version of yourself to consult

USO CHARLOTTE SHOWS SHE'S AWESOME IN ANY REALITY.

with. I knew that had to be bittersweet, which is why Old Mark has outlasted his Abby.

Once I had that, and the idea of Old Mark being the elder statesman to a cadre of Crusaders, I knew I had the end of that fight. I still kept with the "never seeing fights" part of *Love and Capes*. Their appearance was enough.

In that mass of Marks are a bunch of versions based on different Superman stories. Obviously, there had to be a gender swapped version (no doubt from Doctor Karmette's universe) and a different race. The black suit is

THE BRANDON ROUTH HOMAGE VERSION OF THE CRUSADER.

the "Death of Superman" version. There's a cyborg version, one based on the Superman of the Future stories, a funny animal one (based on my cat, Mal) with a pun for a name that made me think it was meant to be. There's a '90s version wearing leather, one with a goatee, one with just a t-shirt. The one without the swoop in his hair is based on the Superman of 2965. There's an Elvis Crusader. And way in the middle back? That's an homage to Brandon Routh. I loved his Superman, and seeing him reprise the role in the DC crossover event and be let go from the show pretty unceremoniously, I wanted to honor him a little bit. I didn't know how much I needed to see his Superman until he reappeared.

The hardest thing was the naming of Hayley. Honestly, she's just named after Hayley Atwell, who I think is awesome. But when the story became a flashback and I realized I could show them naming her… well, I didn't have a good reason. If I'd had a more solid plan, I would have figured out a way to have Old Mark help name her. But that was not to be. A lot of things just fit together, but I'm not always the master planner I appear.

Nope.

# SO IS THIS GOODBYE?

I'm back now. I don't know when or where, but being able to jump ahead in the timeline makes me want to tell more stories. Hayley had her moment in the sun with her birth, but her personailty hasn't come through yet. I want to tell stories about her and who she becomes. About how James grows into following his father's footsteps. I want to tell stories about how Zoe and Paul go forward, and will they have a child? And I want to do a lot more with Charlotte who deserves more than her appearances in this trade.

I abandoned an idea of her getting a teleporting cat or a robot pet. There was no room for it, and it was too similar to the Flerkin in *Captain Marvel*. There's still a lot of pages left in her story that didn't fit in here.

So yeah, I'll see you all… soon.

# LIVING IN A DIGITAL WORLD

In the five years since I last did *Love and Capes,* a lot changed, particularly with how I make art. Previously, I worked traditionally in brush and ink, and only colored and lettered on computer. But in the intervening time, I got a Cintiq and iPad Pro, and the program Clip Studio came along. All of which meant I had transitioned to working digital.

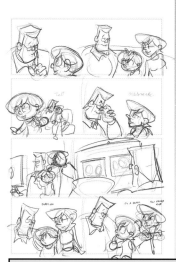

Previously, each page of *Love and Capes* began on a sheet of tracing paper over the Bristol board four tier grid that I'd used since 2006. Art was drawn and redrawn, finally transferred with a lightbox to layout paper, scanned, and then composited with exisiting backgrounds.

Now my grid was digital. For the most part, every page of this version of *Love and Capes* started as a sketch in Procreate on my iPad. Eventually, it was transferred to my iMac Pro and Cintiq, where I tightened and inked the image, exported it to Photoshop and colored it, and finally lettered it in Illustrator.

This new method came with some new restrictions. Before, I usually had lots of bleed area in each panel that allowed me to resize the panel if my dialogue got a little heavy. But now, I had to leave enough room for the dialogue since every panel was drawn to size.

**THE ROUGH LAYOUT OF THE PAGE (PAGE 134 IN THIS COLLECTION), BEGUN ON IPAD.**

Having started my career as a letterer, you'd think that leaving room for copy would be more natural for me, but I'd really come to rely on that crutch of changing the size of art in each panel. So I started off taking the first five pages and finishing them to stress test my system. I eventually got comfortable with it, but it was always on my mind.

I was also conscious that my style had changed, and I had to find a way to merge my existing *Love and Capes* designs with what

**TIGHTER PENCILS DONE IN PROCREATE.**

made sense to me now. You'll see this mostly in proportions and eye size. Hopefully, it blends enough not to be jarring. Of course, even the characters as designed in issue #1 changed along the way. I think this is just the natural progression of an artist and happens in lots of books.

**FINISHED INKS IN CLIP STUDIO. NOTE THE USE OF MULTIPLE COLORED INKLINES FOR BACKGROUND ELEMENTS THAT WOULD BE PRINTED WITH COLORED HOLDING LINES ON THE FINISHED PAGE.**

# "C" IS FOR COOKIE... AND COMIC

A few years ago, I worked with JustJenn recipes to do a Hostess-style print of *Love and Capes*. Up until this volume, this was the only adventure that took place after the end of *Love and Capes: What to Expect.*

There is a mistake in that Zoe should not be wearing her tiara since she was still banished at this point. Whoops! I just didn't think she looked right without some sort of headpiece.

## JUSTJENN RECIPES COMIC CON POWER COOKIES

INGREDIENTS:
2 CUPS ALL-PURPOSE FLOUR
1 TABLESPOON ESPRESSO POWDER
1 TEASPOON BAKING SODA
1/2 TEASPOON KOSHER SALT
1 CUP (2 STICKS) BUTTER, SOFTENED
1 CUP BROWN SUGAR
1/2 CUP WHITE SUGAR
2 TEASPOONS VANILLA
2 EGGS
1 CUP OLD FASHIONED ROLLED OATS
8 OUNCES CHOCOLATE CHIPS

- PREHEAT THE OVEN TO 350 DEGREES AND LINE BAKING SHEETS WITH PARCHMENT.
- IN A LARGE BOWL WHISK TOGETHER THE FLOUR, ESPRESSO POWDER, BAKING SODA AND SALT. SET ASIDE.
- IN THE BOWL OF AN ELECTRIC MIXER CREAM THE BUTTER, BROWN SUGAR AND WHITE SUGAR. ADD THE VANILLA AND THE EGGS UNTIL COMBINED.
- ADD THE FLOUR MIXTURE AND OATS UNTIL THE DOUGH COMES TOGETHER, THEN FOLD IN THE CHOCOLATE CHIPS.
- DROP DOUGH BY ROUNDED TABLESPOON ONTO PREPPED BAKING SHEETS.
- BAKE FOR 10-12 MINUTES UNTIL BROWN, DEPENDING ON YOUR OVEN, AND LET COOL ON A WIRE RACK

@justjenn • www.justjennrecipes.com          @loveandcapes • www.loveandcapes.com

# PRO ART

## ALAN DAVIS ▶

Alan Davis showed his love for *Love and Capes* by sending me this image of the whole Love and Capes crew. I'd chatted with him about doing a blurb for the back cover. I didn't expect this at all. It's amazing, and one of my favorite possessions.

## ◀ JEREMY DALE

The late Jeremy Dale was a friend of mine. We worked together on his book *Skyward*, which I letter. He also did a daily "Skratchaday" drawing post and he chose Mark and Abby as features one day, which was amazing, as well as the first time anyone else had drawn my characters.

## ANDY SMITH ▶

Andy was a year ahead of me at the Kubert School, and we've become friends since then. He's also a fan of the book, and at a particularly slow convention, he did this fantastic piece of the Crusader!

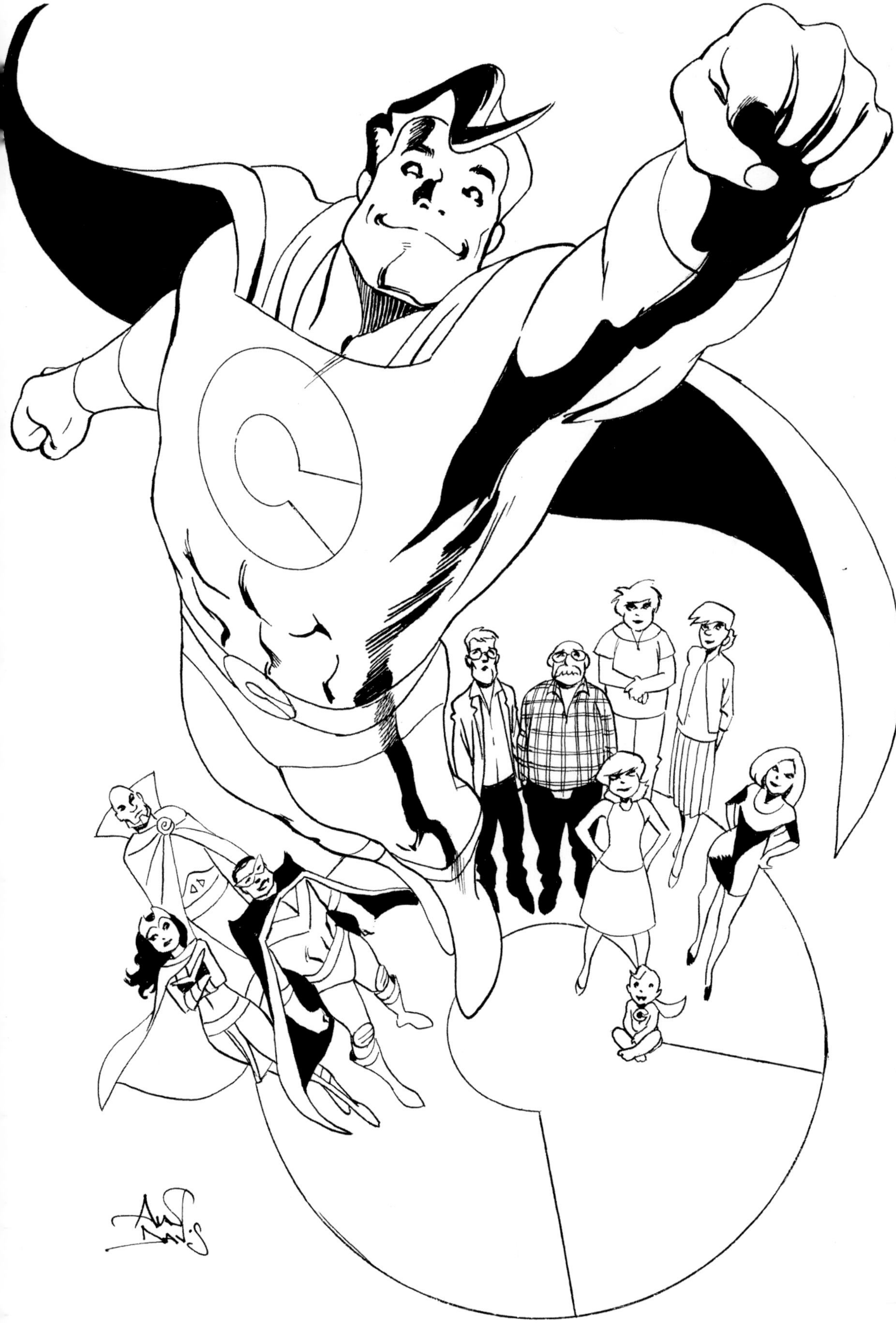

# LOVE AND CAPES

## WRITTEN AND DRAWN BY THOMAS F. ZAHLER

Thom Zahler is just an average, everyday cartoonist. Maybe a little taller than most, but other than that nothing special. He's certainly not part of an international conspiracy that includes the Rand Corporation, the Saucer People, and reverse-vampires.

And there's no secret, subliminal backward masked messages buried in his work from IDW's *Time and Vine* and *Long Distance* to Line WEBTOON'S *Warning Label* and *Cupid's Arrows*.

He just simply grew up in the Catholic Church, went to a secretive art school in New Jersey (allegedly called "The Kubert School"), worked for a newspaper, and was a municipal councilman who swore an oath to uphold the Constitution. How could someone like that not be hired to write *My Little Pony*?

Thom lives in a perfectly normal house in northeast Ohio with no secret rooms, and certainly not in the secret subterranean tunnels underneath the Denver Airport with the lizard people Illuminati.

*Gnky Inky! Ynu ehe ht! Same cm alchk whtg tga suoiaft khzcre panpka tn tz ct tgnl ent fnl tn rafahva c prhza!*

SPECIAL THANKS TO:
AMY WOLFRAM, EMILY WHITTEN, BRIAN WARD,
BILL WILLIAMS, DEITRI VILLARREAL, PAUL D. STORRIE,
JAMES SANTANGELO, JILL A. SMITH,
ROGER PRICE, MARC NATHAN,
JON MONSON-FOON,
JESSE JACKSON, LORA INNES, KARA EVANS,
CARMEN DELUCCIA, LUKE DAAB,
CHRISTY BLANCH, AND
MIKE BOKAUSEK